A Garden of Needlework

Cross Stitch Embroidery For The Home

Edited By: Mary Bartley Stockett

GRAPHWORKS INTERNATIONAL INC. ● NASHVILLE

For Rose
who brings a garden of love to our hearts

Editor
Mary Bartley Stockett

Concept Design Team
Mary Bartley Stockett
David M. Bartley
Rose S. Furniss
Norman B. Brown
Cynthia Green

Technical Production Team
Mary Bartley Stockett
Norman B. Brown
Carole Ballman

Production Assistants

Pat Keever	Angie Medina
Betty Hanner	Paula Elder
Pam Sutphin	Cindy Craig
Bill Hammond	J. Mooneyhan
Darlyne Huggins	

Additional Production Support

Zweigart®

The DMC Corporation	Crescent Cardboard Co.
Susan Bates Inc./Anchor	Anne Brinkley Designs Inc.
Kreinik	Sudberry House Inc.
Offray Ribbon Co.	Wheatland Crafts Inc.
Carol Peeples Cook	

Our warmest appreciation to Mrs. Carol Peeples Cook for extending her gracious hospitality by allowing us to photograph in her home.

Photographs for this publication were taken at Ridge Acres, located in Springfield, Tennessee, thirty miles north of Nashville. The Georgian estate, home of Mrs. Carol Peeples Cook, is in the style of country manor houses in England. The twenty-two room residence is furnished throughout with French and English antiques.

First Published in 1990 by Graphworks International Inc.
400 Old Two Mile Pike Goodlettsville, TN 37072 U.S.A.
(615) 859-1201   FAX:(615) 851-7100
©1990 Graphworks International Inc.
All Rights Reserved
Library of Congress Catalog Number: 90-081882
ISBN: 1-878761-00-5
Manufactured in the United States of America
First Edition May 1990
Needlework Industry Product Code Number: 2955
Publisher and vendor disclaim any and all liability in the use of this publication.

GRAPHWORKS INTERNATIONAL INC.
Mary Bartley Stockett
David M. Bartley
Rose S. Furniss

A Garden of Needlework

GENERAL INSTRUCTIONS FOR COUNTED CROSS STITCH EMBROIDERY
LA BRODERIE AU POINT DE CROIX   ALLGEMEINE ANLEITUNG FUR KREUZSTICHSTICKEREI
INSTRUZIONI PER IL RICAMO A PUNTO CROCE   ALGEMENE INSTRUCTIES VOOR BORDUURWERK IN GETELDE KRUISSTEEK
INSTRUCCIONES GENERALES PARA BORDADOS A PUNTO DE CRUZ SOBRE HILOS

Basic Supplies

Charted Designs
Evenweave Fabric
Tapestry Needle
Six Strand Embroidery Floss
Embroidery Hoop
Embroidery Scissors

1. Find the center of the fabric by folding in half and then in half again.
2. Cut an 18" (45 cm) length of floss. Separate into the needed strands.
3. Locate center of design on the graph by following the arrows.
4. Begin stitching the cross stitches first. When beginning, hold a small length of floss on the back side of the fabric and secure the floss with the first few cross stitches.
5. Stitch from left to right, stitching half of the crosses. Then complete the stitches by crossing back over in the opposite direction.
6. Backstitching and French Knots are done after all cross stitching is completed.

Fournitures de base

Diagramme
Etamine
Aiguille à broder
Coton mouliné à broder (6 brins)
Tambor à broder
Ciseaux à broder

1. Pour déterminer le centre de l'étamine, pliez-la quartre.
2. Coupez une longueur de mouliné a broder de 45 cm. Divisez le fil en conservant le nombre de brins souhaité.
3. Repérez le centre du diagramme grace aux flèches.
4. Commencez d'abord par réaliser les points de croix. Au début, laissez dépasser une petite longueur de fil au revers de l'étamine et glissez-la sous les premiers points de croix.
5. Brodez de gauche à droite en réalisant la premiére barre oblique de chaque croix, puis terminezles croix en brodant de croite à gauche, dans la direction opposée.
6. Effectuez les points de piqúre et les points de noeud après avoir réalisé tous les points de croix.

Wichtigale Materialien

Zählvorlage
Handarbeitszahlstoff
Sticknadel ohne Spilze
Sticktwist
Stickrahmen
Stickschere

1. Den Mittelpunkt festlegen, indem Sie das Gewebe in Längs- und Querrichtung zur Hälfte falten.
2. Den Sticktwist in 50 cm länge faden schneiden und das 6-fädige Garn auf-teilen, wie es die Stickerei jeweils erfordert.
3. Die Pfeile am Rand der Zählvorlage weisen auf die Mitte.
4. Zuerst sticken Sic die Kreuzstiche. Am Aufang auf der Rückseite ein kurzes Stück Stickgarn festhalten und nil den ersten Stichen das fadenende sichern.
5. Von links nach rechts zunächst halbe Kreuzstiche sticken, dann in entgegengesetzter Richtung die Kreuzstiche fertig sticken.
6. Rückstich und Knötchenstich folgen erst, wenn alle Kreuzstichmotive fertig sind.

Materiale Fornito

Schema su carta
Taglio di tessuto
Ago per ricamo
Cotone da ricamo a sei fili
(mouline)
Forbici per ricamo

1. Segnare il centro della tela piegandola a meta' sui due lati.
2. Tagliate dalla matassina di cotone una gugliata lunga circa 50 cm, separando poi i fili necessari per il ricamo.
3. Localizzate il centro dello schema seguendo le frecce stampate sui bordo dello stesso.
4. Iniziate a ricamare utilizzando per primo il punto croce, quando iniziate il ricamo lasciate sui rovescio della tela circa 2 cm di filo, che fermerete sotto i primi punti croce.
5. Ricamate da sinistra a destra mezzo punto croce, quindi completate il punto ritornando nella direzione opposta.
6. Quando avrete completato tutto il punto croce, rifinite il ricamo con il punto nodi ed il punto scritto.

Basis benodigdheden

Teltekening
Quadratisch geweven doek
Borduurnaals
Zes-draads borduurgaren
Borduurring
Borduurschaar

1. Zoek het midden van Uw stof op. Daartoe het doek twee keer in de helft vouwen.
2. Knip een draad van 46 cm van Uw garenstreng af. Splitsehen garen in het aantal draadjes dat U nodig heeft.
3. Bepaal het midden can Uw dessin op de teltekening. (Zig pijlen).
4. Borduur eerst de kruissteken. Als U begint laat U aan de achterkant van de stof een klein stukje van de draad los hangen en zet dat vast met de eerstvolgende kruisjes.
5. Borduur dan eerst halve kruisjes van links naar rechts. Daarna de andere helft van de kruisjes borduren van rechts naar links.
6. Stiksteekjes en franse knopen worden geborduurd als alle kruissteekwerk af is.

Materiales Basicos

Gráfico del dibujo
Tejido de trama uniforme
Aguja de tapiceria
Seda floja de seis dabos
Bastidor de bordar
Tijeras de bordar

1. Buscar el centro del tejido doblándolo por la mitad y luego nueva mente por la mitad.
2. Cortar hebras de seda de 45 cm. Separar los cabos según convenga en cada porción, enhubrando la aguja con los necesarios.
3. Localizer el centro del dibujo del gráfico las flechas.
4. Empezar bordando los puntos de cruz. Al principio, dejar sobre lir por el revés de la labor el extremo del hilo; fijarlo continuación con los primeros puntos de cruz.
5. Procadiendo de izquierda a derecho bordar primero la mitad de las cruces. Luego completar los puntos dando puntadas que crucen la primeras por el centro, procediendo en dirección opuesta.
6. Trabajar el punto de pespunte y los nudos franceses cuando se ha coplatado el punto de cruz.

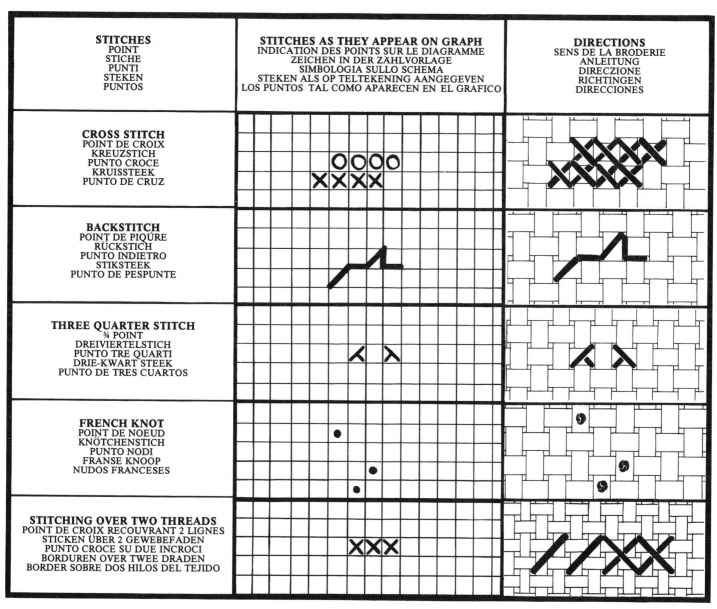

STITCHES POINT STICHE PUNTI STEKEN PUNTOS	STITCHES AS THEY APPEAR ON GRAPH INDICATION DES POINTS SUR LE DIAGRAMME ZEICHEN IN DER ZÄHLVORLAGE SIMBOLOGIA SULLO SCHEMA STEKEN ALS OP TELTEKENING AANGEGEVEN LOS PUNTOS TAL COMO APARECEN EN EL GRAFICO	DIRECTIONS SENS DE LA BRODERIE ANLEITUNG DIRECZIONE RICHTINGEN DIRECCIONES
CROSS STITCH POINT DE CROIX KREUZSTICH PUNTO CROCE KRUISSTEEK PUNTO DE CRUZ		
BACKSTITCH POINT DE PIQÚRE RÜCKSTICH PUNTO INDIETRO STIKSTEEK PUNTO DE PESPUNTE		
THREE QUARTER STITCH ¾ POINT DREIVIERTELSTICH PUNTO TRE QUARTI DRIE-KWART STEEK PUNTO DE TRES CUARTOS		
FRENCH KNOT POINT DE NOEUD KNÖTCHENSTICH PUNTO NODI FRANSE KNOOP NUDOS FRANCESES		
STITCHING OVER TWO THREADS POINT DE CROIX RECOUVRANT 2 LIGNES STICKEN ÜBER 2 GEWEBEFADEN PUNTO CROCE SU DUE INCROCI BORDUREN OVER TWEE DRADEN BORDER SOBRE DOS HILOS DEL TEJIDO		

Credits

Fabrics By: Zweigart®
Clock (photo page 39) By: Sudberry House Inc.
Sofa Table and Pin Cushion (Photo Page 39) By: Wheatland Crafts® Inc.
Porcelain, Metal and Lead Cut Crystal By: Framecraft™ Miniatures Ltd.; Anne Brinkley Designs, Inc.
Mat Boards By: Crescent Mat Board Co.
Frames By: Shenandoah Framing Co., Piedmont Moulding Co., Wheatland Crafts® Inc., Nielsen Moulding (U.S.A)
Balger® Filaments and Metallics By: Kreinik
Fil or clair and Fil argent clair By: The DMC Corporation
Embroidery Flosses By: The DMC Corporation and Susan Bates/Anchor
Ribbons By: Offray Ribbon Co.
Marlitt Floss By: Zweigart®
Photography By: Wölf Flöege-Böehm, International Photo Haus

For information in locating any of the products listed in this publication, please contact:

Graphworks International Inc.
P.O. Box 352   400 Old Two Mile Pike   Goodlettsville, TN 37072 U.S.A.
(615) 859-1201   FAX: (615) 851-7100   1-800-826-1998

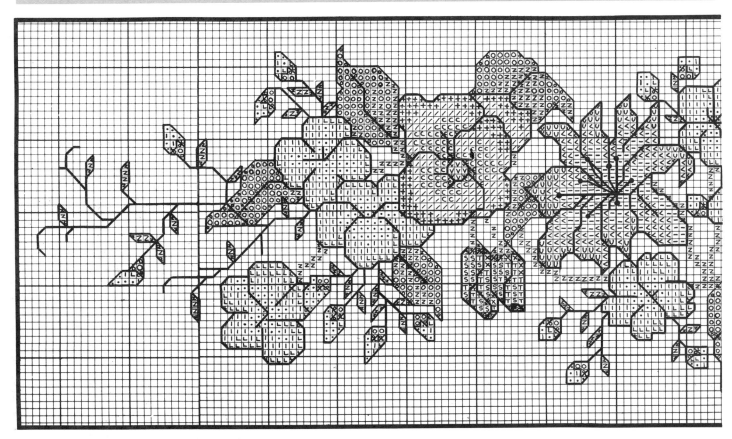

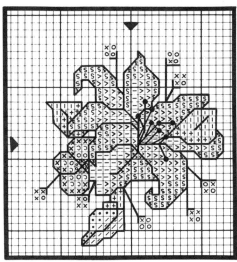

Heart Box

	DMC	ANCHOR	COLOR
/	776	24	Baby Pink
•	899	27	Dark Baby Pink
o	775	128	Very Light Baby Blue
⊃	3325	159	Light Baby Blue
×	334	145	Baby Blue
I	470	267	Avocado Green
+	890	879	Very Dark Soft Green
>	742	303	Light Tangerine
–	740	316	Dark Tangerine
S	743	297	Dark Yellow
	801	357	Dark Brown

Backstitch stems of flowers in Very Dark Soft Green. (2 strands)
Make long straight stitches using 2 strands of Dark Brown to make the pistils of the flowers. Then make small French Knots using Dark Brown to make the stamens at the tips of the pistils.
All other backstitching is in Dark Brown.

Zweigart® Jubilee 28 Ct. Pink/Lavender
Floss Skeins
26 Tapestry Needle
Embroidery Hoop (optional)

Use 2 strands for cross stitching
Use 1 strand for backstitching
(unless otherwise indicated)
Stitch Over Two (to make 14 Ct.)
Cut Fabric Size: 8" (20.3 cm) x 8" (20.3 cm)

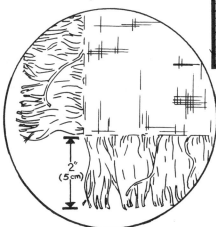

2"
(5 cm)

Fringe edges of
vanity scarf
to finish

Powder Box

	DMC	ANCHOR	COLOR
/	776	24	Baby Pink
•	899	27	Dark Baby Pink
v	335	42	Light Carnation Red
o	775	128	Very Light Baby Blue
c	3225	159	Light Baby Blue
×	334	145	Baby Blue
I	470	267	Avocado Green
+	890	879	Very Dark Soft Green
	801	357	Dark Brown

Backstitch stems of flowers in Very Dark Soft Green. (2 strands)
All other backstitching is in Dark Brown.

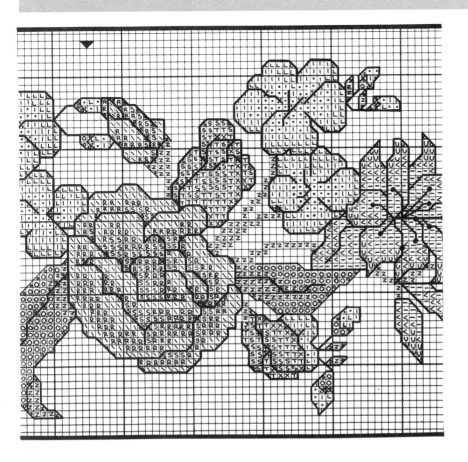

Legend

DMC	ANCHOR	COLOR
• 775	128	Very Light Baby Blue
I 3325	159	Light Baby Blue
V 725	306	Dark Topaz Yellow
T 335	42	Light Carnation Red
X 326	59	Dark Carnation Red
L 334	145	Baby Blue
O 3346	257	Hunter Green
Z 895	246	Dark Hunter Green
C 550	102	Dark Violet
U 743	297	Dark Yellow
+ 211	108	Light Lavender
/ 209	105	Lavender
< 742	303	Light Tangerine
— 740	316	Dark Tangerine
\ 819	892	Light Baby Pink
R 776	24	Baby Pink
S 899	27	Dark Baby Pink
938	381	Very Dark Brown

Backstitch stems of flowers in Dark Hunter Green.

Make long straight stitches using 1 strand of Very Dark Brown to make the pistils of the flowers.

Make small French Knots using Very Dark Brown to make the stamens at the tips of the pistils.

All other backstitching is in Very Dark Brown.

Materials

Zweigart® Annabelle 28 Ct. White
Floss Skeins
26 Tapestry Needle
Embroidery Hoop (optional)

Specifications

Use 2 strands for cross stitching
Use 1 strand for backstitching
(unless otherwise indicated)
Stitch Over Two (to make 14 Ct.)
Stitch Count: 216w x 50h
Design Area Size: 15½" (39.4) x 3½" (8.9 cm)
Cut Fabric Size: 23½" (59.7 cm) x 11½" (29.2 cm)
(allows 4" (10 cm) on all sides)

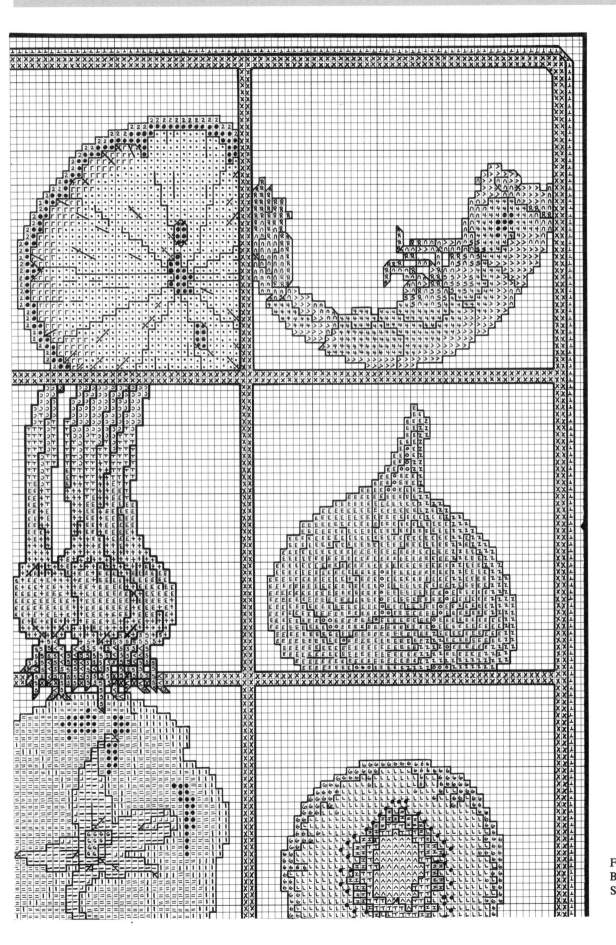

For legend of
Bon Appetit
See Page 13.

1.

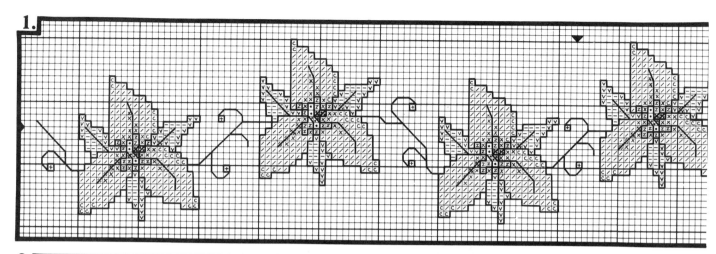

2.

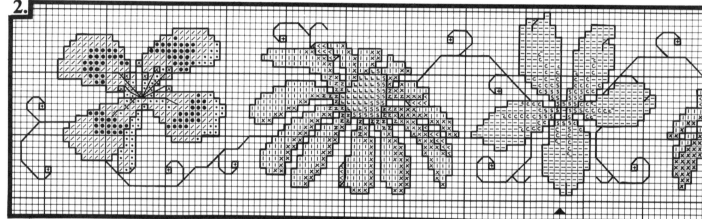

1.

	DMC	ANCHOR	COLOR
−	3364	843	Light Pine Green
V	3362	862	Dark Pine Green
X	327	101	Antique Violet
∕	3608	86	Plum Pink
C	3607	87	Dark Plum Pink
Z	3354	74	Dusty Rose
+	907	255	Light Bright Green
•	3770	892	Light Rose Beige
	844	401	Very Dark Grey
	987	244	Forest Green

Towels are cross stitched using 3 strands of
floss, and backstitched using 2 strands.
Backstitch flowers are in Very Dark Grey.
Backstitch leaves and vines between flowers
in Forest Green.

Zweigart® Gourmet Kitchen Towels 10 Ct. Hearts
Pink/Blue
Floss Skeins
24 Tapestry Needle
Embroidery Hoop (optional)

Use 3 strands for cross stitching
Use 2 strands for backstitching
(unless otherwise indicated)
Stitch Count: 181w x 29h
Towel Size: 18" (45.7 cm) x 26" (66 cm)
Cut Fabric Size: 20" (50.8 cm) x 28" (71.1 cm)
(allows 1" double fold hem seam on all sides)

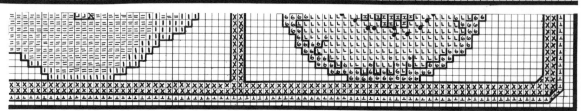

LEFT BOTTOM

RIGHT BOTTOM

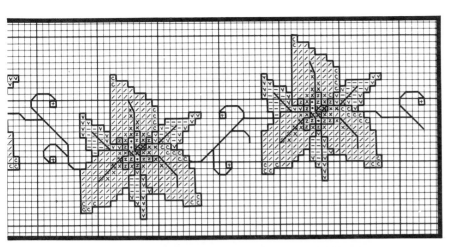

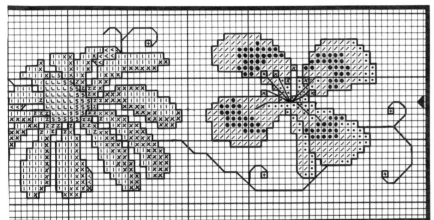

Legend

Bon Appétit

	DMC	ANCHOR	COLOR
X	992	187	Teal Green
⊥	991	189	Dark Teal Green
V	727	293	Light Topaz Yellow
H	726	295	Topaz Yellow
N	581	266	Moss Green
‖	580	267	Dark Moss Green
∧	472	264	Very Light Avocado Green
L	471	266	Light Avocado Green
6	469	267	Avocado Green
I	935	862	Dark Avocado Green
c	989	242	Light Forest Green
8	986	246	Dark Forest Green
Ⅎ	907	255	Bright Green
/	712	387	Off White
3	834	874	Green Gold
z	739	885	Very Light Tan
<	436	363	Dark Tan
9	976	308	Cinnamon
⊢	842	376	Light Beige Brown
P	839	380	Dark Beige Brown
U	762	397	Very Light Grey
S	415	398	Light Grey
2	744	301	Baby Yellow
•	743	297	Dark Baby Yellow
●	White	2	White
Γ	445	288	Light Lemon Yellow
R	922	324	Very Light Rust Red
T	702	256	Light Green
⊃	702	239	Green
4	948	778	Very Light Peach
⊅	353	8	Peach
∩	352	10	Dark Peach
+	677	886	Very Light Old Gold
5	729	890	Old Gold
E	746	386	Soft White
I	349	13	Dark Coral Red
=	606	335	Burnt Orange
⊣	913	209	Light Mint Green
–	909	229	Dark Mint Green
ɢ	300	352	Dark Rust Brown
o	224	893	Light Shell Pink
	221	897	Dark Shell Pink
	741	304	Tangerine
	3371	382	Black Brown

Make French Knots for Kiwi Fruit in Black Brown.
Backstitch lettering is in Teal Green.
Note: When backstitching food, use 1 strand for the outline and 2 strands for the inside, unless otherwise indicated.
Backstitch the mushroom slice in Dark Beige Brown. (1 strand, outline) and Very Light Beige Brown (2 strands, inside).
Backstitch lemon slice in Tangerine (1 strand, outline, 2 strands, inside).

(continued at bottom left of this page)

2. *DMC ANCHOR COLOR*

	DMC	ANCHOR	COLOR
/	776	24	Baby Pink
•	899	27	Dark Baby Pink
●	3706	28	Melon Pink
I	211	108	Very Light Lavender
X	210	104	Light Lavender
Z	340	118	Blue Violet
<	3607	87	Dark Plum Pink
L	676	891	Light Old Gold
S	729	890	Old Gold
–	745	300	Light Yellow
C	743	297	Dark Yellow
+	992	187	Teal Green
	333	119	Dark Blue Violet
	3022	8581	Grey Brown
	781	309	Topaz Gold

Towels are cross stitched using 3 strands of floss, and backstitched using 2 strands.
Backstitch stems in Teal Green.
Backstitch pink flowers in Grey Brown.
Backstitch lavender flowers in Dark Blue Violet.
Backstitch yellow flower in Topaz Gold.

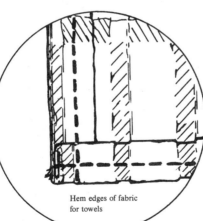

Hem edges of fabric for towels

(continued)
Backstitch shrimp in Very Light Rust Red (1 strand, outline, 2 strands, inside)
Backstitch egg slice in Light Green Gold (2 strands).
Backstitch garlic clove in Dark Shell Pink.
Backstitch tomato in Dark Rust Brown (1 strand, outline, 2 strands, inside).
Backstitch Kiwi Fruit slice in Very Dark Avocado Green (1 strand, outline, 2 strand, inside).
Backstitch box frame in Black Brown.
All other backstitching is in Black Brown (1 strand, outline, 2 strands, inside).

Materials

Zweigart® Lugana 25 Ct. Cream
Floss Skeins
26 Tapestry Needle
Embroidery Hoop (optional)

Specifications

Use 2 strands for cross stitching
Use 1 strand for backstitching
(unless otherwise indicated)
Stitch Over Two (to make 12½ Ct.)
Stitch Count: 190w x 140h
Design Area Size: 15¼" (38.7 cm) x 11¼" (28.6 cm)
Cut Fabric Size: 23¼" (59 cm) x 19¼" (48.9 cm)
(allows 4" (10 cm) on all sides)

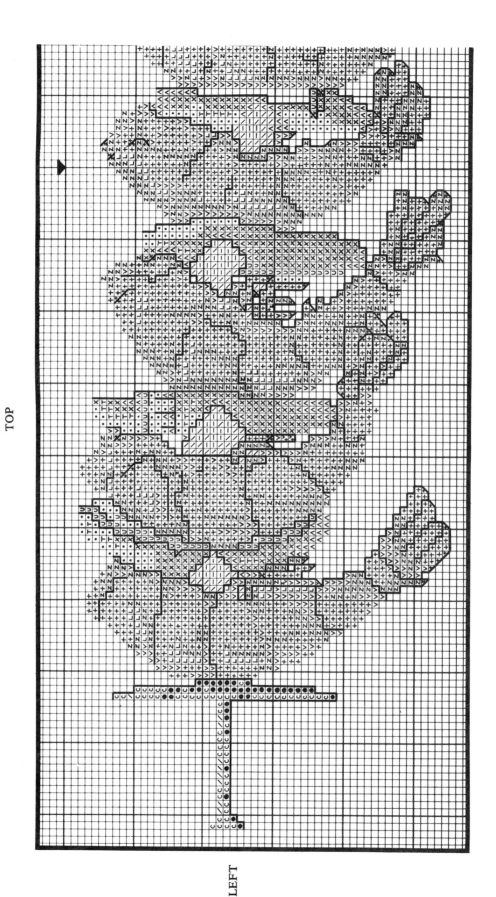

TOP

LEFT

RIGHT

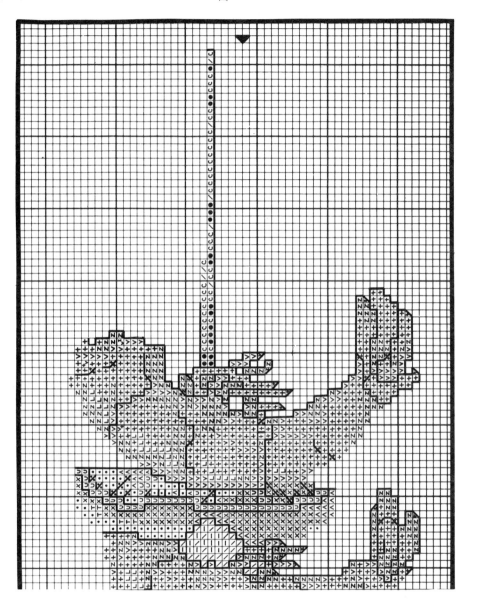

Legend

DMC	ANCHOR	COLOR
∕	762	397	Light Steel Grey
C	318	399	Steel Grey
●	414	400	Dark Steel Grey
+	402	347	Light Rust Brown
Z	922	324	Light Rust Red
V	920	339	Rust Red
L	948	778	Light Peach
T	445	288	Light Lemon Yellow
·	307	289	Lemon Yellow
X	444	291	Dark Lemon Yellow
U	744	301	Yellow
—	703	238	Light Green
\	700	229	Dark Green
∧	742	303	Light Tangerine
	740	316	Dark Tangerine
	840	379	Beige Brown

Lemon is backstitched in Dk. Tangerine.
All other backstitching is in Beige Brown.

Materials

Zweigart® Lugana 25 Ct. White
Floss Skeins
26 Tapestry Needle
Embroidery Hoop (optional)

Specifications

Use 2 strands for cross stitching
Use 1 strand for backstitching
(unless otherwise indicated)
Stitch Over Two (to make 12½ Ct.)
Stitch Count: 184w x 53h
Design Area Size: 14¾" (37.5 cm) x 4¼" (10.8 cm)
Cut Fabric Size: 22¾"(57.8 cm) x 12¼" (31 cm)
(allows 4" (10 cm) on all sides)

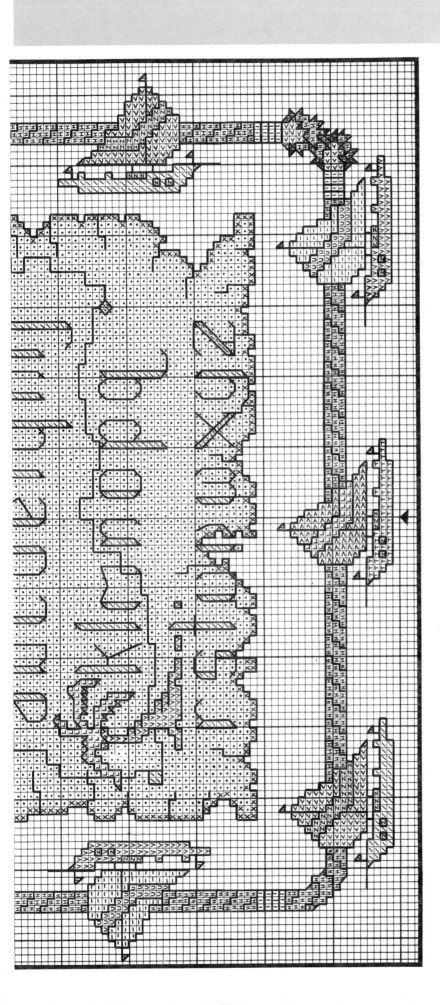

DMC	ANCHOR	COLOR
• 3047	886	Light Straw Gold
✕ 3045	373	Dark Straw Gold
/ 434	309	Light Brown
+ 3371	382	Black Brown
V 922	324	Light Rust Red
T 920	339	Rust Red
U 932	920	Light Antique Blue
− 3033	388	Very Light Mocha Brown
L 907	255	Light Bright Green
> 745	300	Light Yellow
Z 743	297	Dark Yellow
I 666	46	Bright Red
< 739	885	Very Light Tan
H 738	942	Light Tan

Backstitch ship's anchor in Bright Red.
Backstitch rope border in Light Brown.
Backstitch bottle outline in Light Antique Blue.
Use long, straight running stitches for mast
lines connecting sails on ship after all other
cross stitching has been done using Black Brown.
All other backstitching is in Black Brown.

Materials

Zweigart® Aida 14 Ct. Ivory
Floss Skeins
24 Tapestry Needle
Embroidery Hoop (optional)

Specifications

Use 2 strands for cross stitching
Use 1 strand for backstitching
(unless otherwise indicated)
Stitch Count: 126w x 156h
Design Area Size: 9" (22.9 cm) x 11⅛" (28.3 cm)
Cut Fabric Size: 17" (43.2 cm) x 19⅛" (48.6 cm)
(allows 4" (10 cm) on all sides)

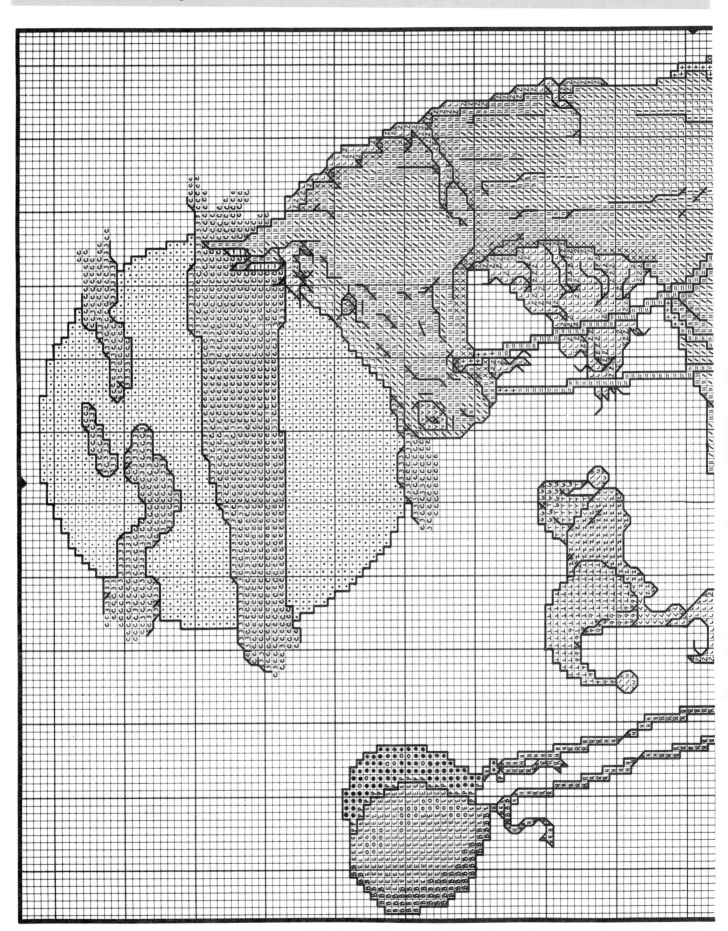

18

Legend

DMC	ANCHOR	COLOR
• 726	295	Topaz Yellow
c 746	386	Soft White
3 3033	388	Very Light Mocha Brown
v 3031	905	Dark Mocha Brown
‖ 435	369	Very Light Brown
x 434	309	Light Brown
∕ 436	363	Dark Tan
⌐ 948	778	Very Light Peach
— 754	8	Light Peach
L 676	891	Light Old Gold
2 729	890	Old Gold
o White	2	White
∧ 3021	382	Dark Grey Brown
⌐ 739	885	Very Light Tan
I 738	942	Light Tan
= 611	898	Bark Brown
+ 610	889	Dark Bark Brown
E 893	27	Bright Pink
B 891	35	Dark Bright Pink
● 211	108	Light Lavender
P 210	104	Lavender
R 762	397	Very Light Steel Grey
H 318	399	Steel Grey
⊥ 959	186	Seagreen
9 958	187	Dark Seagreen
\ 745	300	Light Yellow
U 743	297	Dark Yellow
6 598	167	Light Turquoise
T 597	168	Turquoise
Z 312	147	Very Light Navy Blue
< 311	149	Light Navy Blue
> 310	403	Black
S 844	401	Very Dark Grey

All backstitching is in Dark Grey Brown.
Note: This design is stitched over two threads except for the Jester's face which is stitched over one thread to give greater detail. You must use a linen type weave fabric. An Aida fabric will not allow you to complete the two types of stitching (over one and over two).

Materials

Zweigart® Lugana 25 Ct. Peach
Floss Skeins
26 Tapestry Needle
Embroidery Hoop (optional)

Specifications

Use 2 strands for cross stitching
Use 1 strand for backstitching
(unless otherwise indicated)
Stitch Over Two (to make 12½ Ct.)
Stitch Count: 118w x 187h
Design Area Size: 9½" (24 cm) x 15" (38 cm)
Cut Fabric Size: 17½" (44.4 cm) x 23" (58.4 cm)
(allows 4" (10 cm) on all sides)

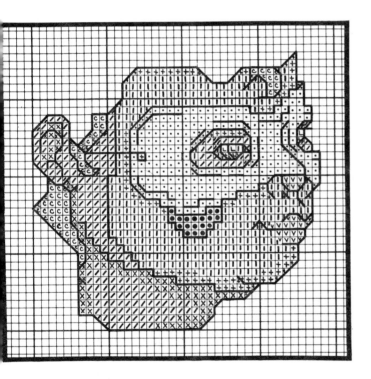

Jester's Face

DMC	ANCHOR	COLOR
+ 3033	388	Light Mocha Brown
I White	2	White
c 918	341	Very Dark Rust Red
∕ 948	778	Very Light Peach
x 754	778	Light Peach
● 351	11	Light Coral Red
· 844	401	Very Dark Grey
L 806	169	Ocean Blue
v 335	42	Light Carnation Red
3021	382	Dark Grey Brown

All backstitching is in Dark Grey Brown.

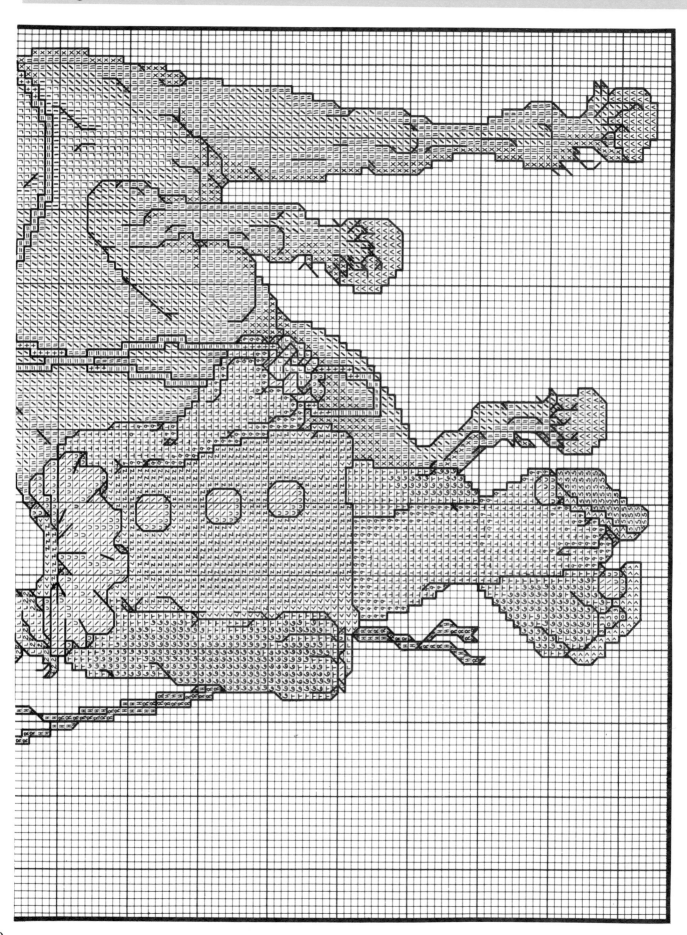

Legend

1

	DMC	ANCHOR	COLOR
•	818	48	Light Baby Pink
X	776	24	Baby Pink
C	335	42	Carnation Red
V	892	28	Bright Pink
O	349	13	Dark Coral Red
/	350	11	Coral Red
I	899	27	Dark Baby Pink
<	3348	265	Light Hunter Green
+	3347	266	Hunter Green
U	3346	257	Dark Hunter Green
S	470	267	Avocado Green
	890	879	Dark Soft Green
	3685	70	Dark Mauve Red

Backstitch flower in Dark Mauve Red.
Backstitch leaves in Dark Soft Green.

2

	DMC	ANCHOR	COLOR
•	3078	292	Baby Yellow
+	3072	397	Light Pearl Grey
X	3608	86	Plum Pink
/	211	108	Lavender
C	472	264	Avocado Green
V	906	256	Bright Green
O	973	920	Canary Yellow
	844	401	Very Dark Grey

Backstitching is in Very Dark Grey.

3

	DMC	ANCHOR	COLOR
•	3747	120	Periwinkle
X	553	98	Violet
●	333	119	Blue Violet
C	727	293	Topaz Yellow
V	3052	859	Grey Green
I	3051	846	Dark Grey Green

Backstitch short lines on each side in Topaz Yellow.
All other backstitching is in Blue Violet.

4

	DMC	ANCHOR	COLOR
V	223	894	Shell Pink
/	3770	892	Rose Beige
C	3685	70	Dark Mauve Red
X	3347	266	Hunter Green

Backstitch flower petals in Shell Pink.
Backstitch stamen in Dark Mauve Red.
French Knots are in Dark Mauve Red. (2 strands)

Materials

Zweigart® Annabelle 28 Ct. White/Pink/Blue
Floss Skeins
26 Tapestry Needle
Embroidery Hoop (optional)

Specifications

Use 2 strands for cross stitching
Use 1 strand for backstitching
(unless otherwise indicated)
Stitch Over Two (to make 14 Ct.)
Flowers 5 and 6 are shown stitched over one
Cut Fabric Size: 8" (20.3 cm) x 8" (20.3 cm)

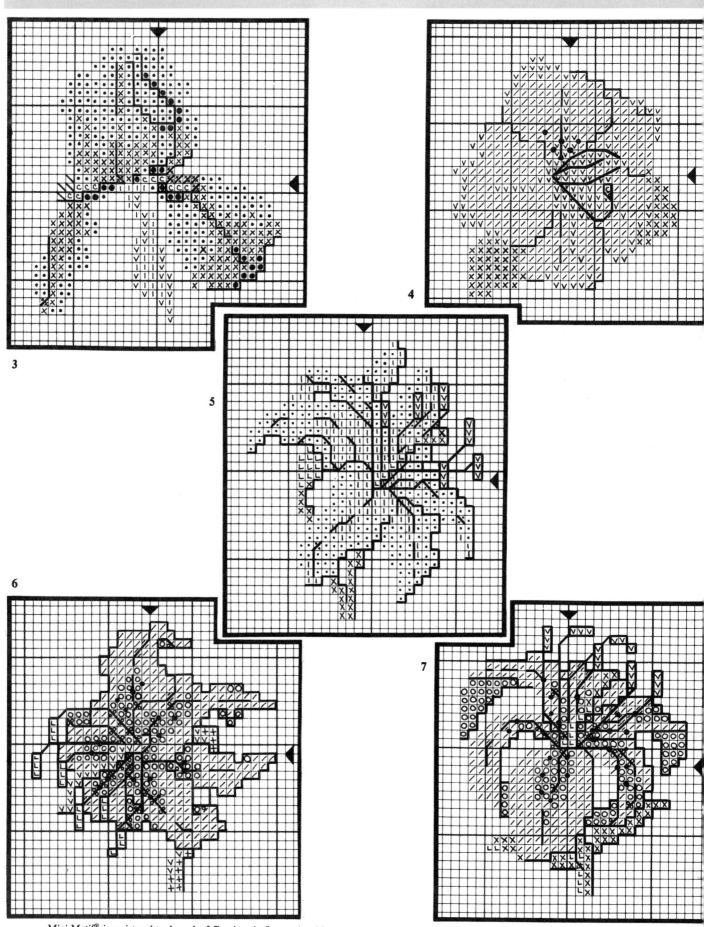

Mini Motif® is registered trademark of Graphworks International Inc.

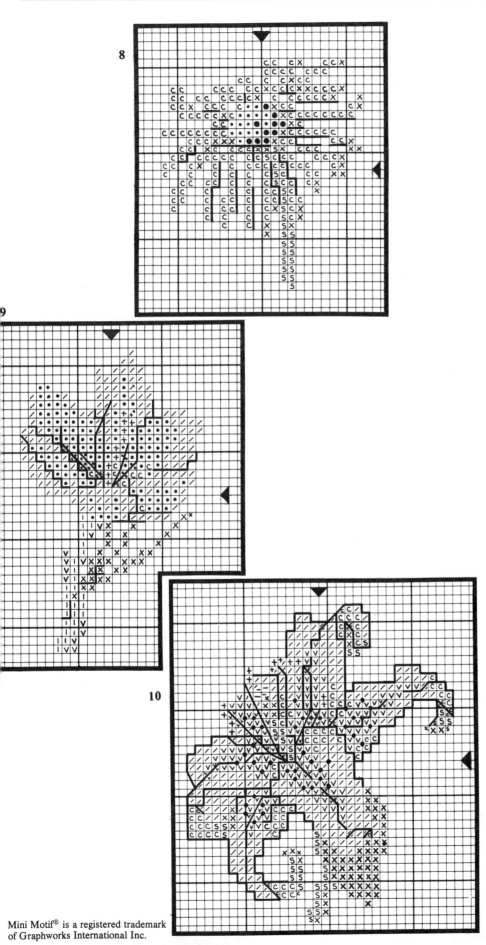

5

DMC	ANCHOR	COLOR	
V	301	349	Rust
I	3608	86	Plum Pink
•	341	117	Light Blue Violet
L	955	241	Light Green
X	988	243	Dark Green
	844	401	Very Dark Grey

Long straight strands for pistils are in Dark Green.
All other backstitching is in Very Dark Grey.

6

DMC	ANCHOR	COLOR	
L	301	349	Rust
/	White	2	White
O	3689	49	Light Mauve Pink
V	704	256	Light Green
+	702	239	Dark Green
	3688	66	Mauve Pink
	3033	388	Light Mocha Brown
	610	889	Bark Brown

French Knots are in Mauve Pink. (2 strands)
Long straight strands for pistils are in Light Green.
Backstitch indicated on graph in broken dotted
line is in Light Mocha Brown.
All other backstitching is in Bark Brown.

7

DMC	ANCHOR	COLOR	
/·	3078	292	Light Yellow
O	743	305	Dark Yellow
L	955	241	Light Green
X	988	243	Dark Green
V	301	349	Rust
	310	403	Black
	3032	903	Mocha Brown

French Knots are in Black. (2 strands)
Long straight strands for pistils are in Dark Green.
All other backstitching is in Mocha Brown.

8

DMC	ANCHOR	COLOR	
C	3716	74	Light Mauve
X	3731	76	Dark Mauve
•	743	297	Yellow
●	783	307	Topaz Gold
S	954	203	Mint Green

Backstitching is in Dark Mauve.

9

DMC	ANCHOR	COLOR	
/	727	293	Topaz Yellow
•	742	303	Tangerine
+	720	326	Pumpkin
C	921	349	Rust Red
V	906	256	Bright Green
X	904	258	Dark Bright Green
I	471	266	Avocado Green

Backstitch stamen in Pumpkin.
Backstitch flower in Rust Red.
Backstitch stem in Dark Bright Green.

10

DMC	ANCHOR	COLOR	
/	White	2	White
C	415	398	Light Steel Grey
·V	3689	49	Light Mauve Red
−	745	300	Yellow
+	921	349	Rust Red
X	702	239	Christmas Green
S	472	264	Avocado Green
	3687	69	Dark Mauve Red
	927	849	Blue Grey

French Knots are in Dark Mauve Red. (2 strands)
Backstitch veins in petals in Dark Mauve Red.
All other backstitching is in Blue Grey.

English Floral Vase

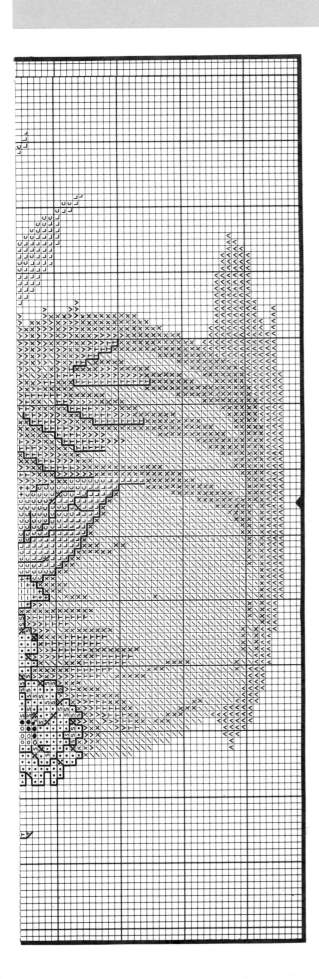

Legend

	DMC	ANCHOR	COLOR
/	356	5975	Brick Red
X	355	5968	Dark Brick Red
O	745	300	Light Yellow
●	744	301	Yellow
B	743	297	Dark Yellow
L	470	267	Avocado Green
C	469	268	Dark Avocado Green
Z	937	268	Very Dark Avocado Green
T	3347	266	Light Hunter Green
V	3346	257	Hunter Green
\	733	280	Light Earth Green
<	732	281	Earth Green
6	894	26	Light Bright Pink
3	893	27	Bright Pink
−	3609	85	Light Plum Pink
+	3608	86	Plum Pink
U	3607	87	Dark Plum Pink
•	white	2	White
S	762	397	Very Light Steel Grey
E	351	11	Light Coral Red
2	349	13	Dark Coral Red
9	352	10	Dark Peach
R	742	303	Light Tangerine
N	341	117	Light Blue Violet
I	340	118	Blue Violet
⊃	333	119	Dark Blue Violet
>	327	101	Dark Antique Violet
G	676	891	Light Old Gold
II	725	306	Dark Topaz Yellow
I	827	159	Very Light True Blue
=	813	160	Light True Blue
∧	928	900	Light Blue Grey
	318	399	Steel Grey
	826	161	True Blue
	350	11	Coral Red

Backstitch white flowers in Steel Grey.
Backstitch center of blue flowers in True Blue.
Backstitch purple Zinna in Dark Blue Violet.
Backstitch highlights of Tiger Lily in Dark
Antique Violet.
Backstitch veins and highlights of leaves in
Very Dark Avocado Green.
Backstitch highlights of coral flowers in Coral
Red.
Backstitch Bouncing Bets in Bright Pink.

Materials

Zweigart® Lugana 25 Ct. White
Floss Skeins
26 Tapestry Needle
Embroidery Hoop (optional)

Specifications

Use 2 strands for cross stitching
Use 1 strand for backstitching
(unless otherwise indicated)
Stitch Over Two (to make 12½ Ct.)
Stitch Count: 132w x 152h
Design Area Size: 10½" (26.7 cm) x 12" (30.5 cm)
Cut Fabric Size: 18½" (47 cm) x 20" (50.8 cm)
(allows 4" (10 cm) on all sides)

25

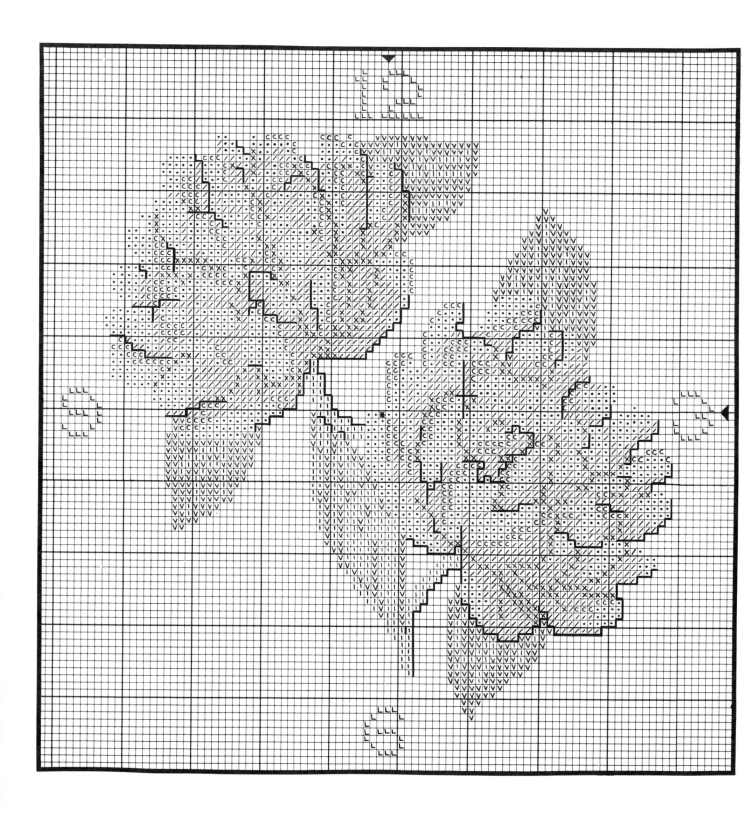

The Peony Clock, Sofa Table and Pin Cushion all use the legend below

	DMC	ANCHOR	COLOR
C	712	387	Ecru
•	963	49	Light Dusty Mauve Pink
/	3688	66	Mauve Pink
X	315	896	Dark Antique Mauve
I	3364	843	Light Pine Green
V	3363	861	Pine Green
L	3362	862	Dark Pine Green [1]
	3350	42	Dark Dusty Rose

Backstitch flower petals in Dark Dusty Rose.
Backstitch stems in Pine Green.

[1] not used in Pin Cushion

* indicates center for mounting clock hands on the Peony clock.

Note: The Sofa Table used the same basic design as the clock. The following changes would need to be made:
1. Eliminate the numbers.
2. Repeat the design every other one turned upside down, five times. See the illustration on this page.

You may repeat this design, reduce or enlarge it by choice of fabric count and use it for pillows, wall hangings, end tables, etc.

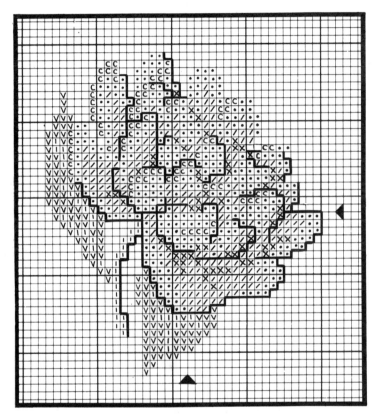

Peony Sofa Table

Zweigart® Lugana 25 Ct. White
Floss Skeins
26 Tapestry Needle
Embroidery Hoop (optional)

Use 2 strands for cross stitching
Use 1 strand for backstitching
(unless otherwise indicated)
Stitch Over Two (to make 12½ Ct.)
Stitch Count: 434w x 81h
Design Area Size: 34¾" (88.3 cm) x 6½" 16.5 cm)
Cut Fabric Size: 42¾" (39 m) x 14½" (36.8 cm)
(allows 4" (10 cm) on all sides)

Peony Pin Cushion

Zweigart® Lugana 25 Ct. White
Floss Skeins
26 Tapestry Needle
Embroidery hoop (optional)

Use 2 strands for cross stitching
Use 1 strand for backstitching
(unless otherwise indicated)
Stitch Over Two (to make 12½ Ct.)
Stitch Count: 37w x 42h
Design Area Size: 3" (7.6 cm x 3⅜" (8.6 cm)
Cut Fabric Size: 11" (28 cm) x 11⅜" (28.9 cm)
(allows 4" (10 cm) on all sides)

Materials

Zweigart® Lugana 25 Ct. White
Floss Skeins
26 Tapestry Needle
Embroidery Hoop (optional)

Specifications

Use 2 strands for cross stitching
Use 1 strand for backstitching
(unless otherwise indicated)
Stitch Over Two (to make 12½ Ct.)
Stitch Count: 94w x 95h
Design Area Size: 7½" (19 cm) x 7⅝" (19.4 cm)
Cut Fabric Size: 15½" (39.4 cm) x 15⅝" (39.7 cm)
(allows 4" (10 cm) on all sides)

Stitch flowers on fabric as is
indicated in illustration below.

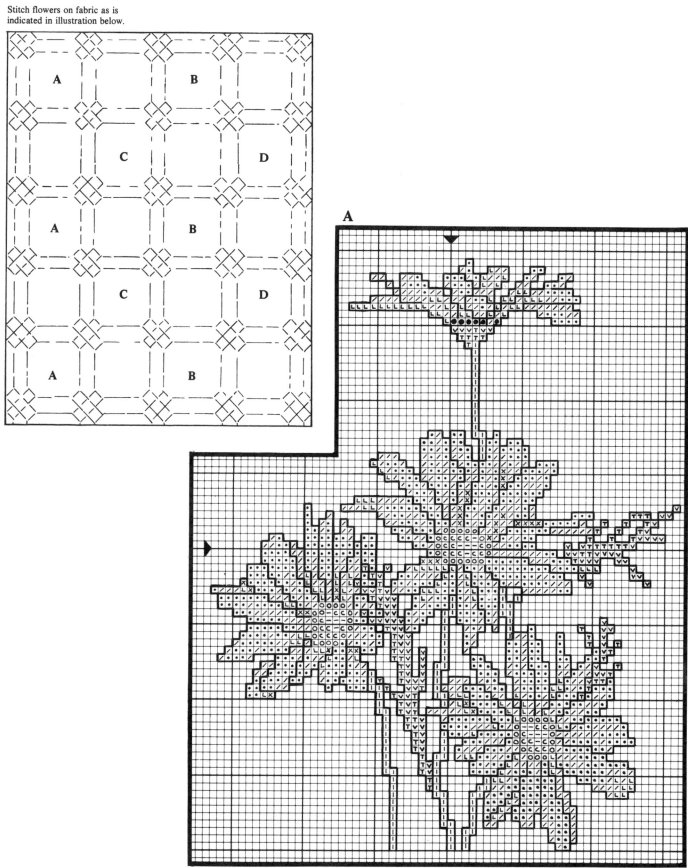

Legend

Daisies   **A**

	DMC	ANCHOR	COLOR
•	White	2	White
●	301	349	Light Rust Brown
—	727	293	Light Topaz Yellow
C	726	295	Topaz Yellow
O	725	306	Dark Topaz Yellow
I	472	264	Very Light Avocado Green
V	471	266	Light Avocado Green
T	470	267	Avocado Green
/	762	397	Very Light Steel Grey
L	415	398	Light Steel Grey
X	318	399	Steel Grey
	469	268	Dark Avocado Green
	317	400	Dark Steel Grey

Backstitch stems in Dark Avocado Green.
Backstitch daisy petals in Dark Steel Grey.

Lily   **B**

	DMC	ANCHOR	COLOR
/	White	2	White
V	819	892	Very Light Baby Pink
+	818	48	Light Baby Pink
S	776	24	Baby Pink
C	899	27	Dark Baby Pink
—	762	397	Very Light Steel Grey
Z	415	398	Light Steel Grey
X	318	399	Steel Grey
I	335	42	Light Carnation Red
O	309	43	Carnation Red
<	347	13	Very Dark Salmon Pink
U	472	264	Very Light Avocado Green
L	471	266	Light Avocado Green
T	470	267	Avocado Green
\	369	213	Ultra Light Soft Green
>	368	240	Very Light Soft Green
H	320	216	Light Soft Green
R	367	246	Soft Green
	844	401	Very Dark Steel Grey

Backstitch stamen of Lily in Carnation Red.
Backstitch leaves and stem in Very Dark Soft Green.
Backstitch petals in Dark Steel Grey.
A small dot on the graph indicates the use of a French Knot using Carnation Red.

Materials

Zweigart® Honeybee 14 Ct. White
Floss Skeins
24 Tapestry Needle
Embroidery hoop (optional)

Specifications

Use 3 strands for cross stitching
Use 2 strands for backstitching
Finished Size: 40¼" (102.2 cm) x 51½" (130.8 cm)

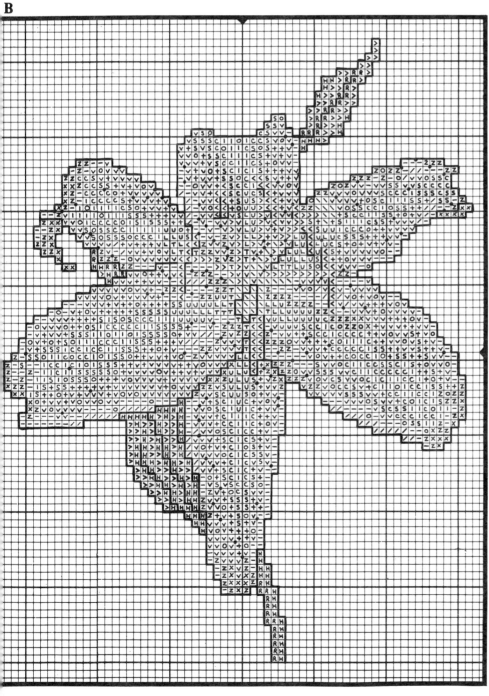

C

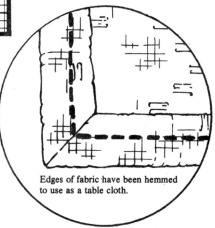

Edges of fabric have been hemmed
to use as a table cloth.

Legend

Chrysanthemum   C

	DMC	ANCHOR	COLOR
·	350	11	Coral Red
C	817	19	Very Dark Coral Red
X	920	339	Rust Red
/	973	920	Canary Yellow
V	972	298	Orange Yellow
+	783	307	Light Topaz Yellow
−	725	306	Dark Topaz Yellow
>	772	264	Very Light Pine Green
T	3364	843	Light Pine Green
L	3363	861	Pine Green

D

China Astor   D

	DMC	ANCHOR	COLOR
O	211	108	Very Light Lavender
U	210	104	Light Lavender
Z	208	110	Dark Lavender
L	800	128	Very Light Cornflower Blue
+	799	130	Light Cornflower Blue
R	798	131	Cornflower Blue
·	3354	74	Dusty Rose
X	3350	42	Dark Dusty Rose
C	961	76	Dark Dusty Pink
I	472	264	Very Light Avocado Green
V	471	266	Light Avocado Green
T	470	267	Avocado Green
>	738	942	Light Tan
H	437	362	Tan
●	369	213	Light Soft Green
/	783	307	Light Topaz Gold
−	727	293	Light Topaz Yellow
<	726	295	Topaz Yellow
	937	268	Very Dark Avocado Green

All backstitching is in Very Dark Avocado Green.

Materials

See Page 29

Specifications

See Page 29

(graph continued on Page 49)

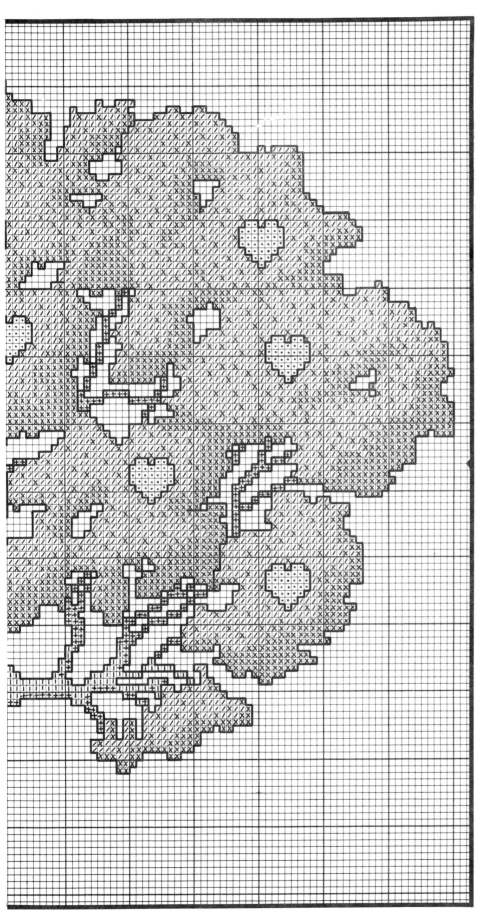

Legend

Anniversary Tree

	DMC	ANCHOR	COLOR
∕	3347	266	Light Hunter Green
X	3345	268	Dark Hunter Green
•	309	42	Carnation Red
+	434	309	Light Brown
I	436	363	Dark Tan
	844	401	Very Dark Grey

Letters and numbers have been provided for personalization.
Backstitch lettering in Carnation Red (2 strands).
Center names above design, then center anniversary number and date below design.
Use scratch sheet of graph paper to practice centering letters.
All other backstitching is in Very Dark Grey.

See pages 52 and 53 for Alphabet.

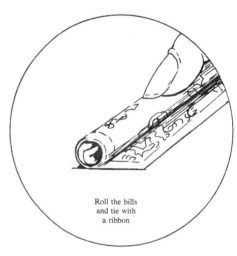

Roll the bills
and tie with
a ribbon

Materials

Zweigart® Lugana 25 Ct. Cream
Floss Skeins
26 Tapestry Needle
Embroidery hoop (optional)

Specifications

Use 2 strands for cross stitching
Use 1 strand for backstitching
(unless otherwise indicated)
Stitch Over Two (to make 12½ Ct.)
Stitch Count: 175w x 209h
Design Area Size: 14" (35.6 cm) x 13½" (34.3 cm)
Cut Fabric Size: 22" (55.9 cm) x 21½" (54.6 cm)
(allows 4" (10 cm) on all sides)

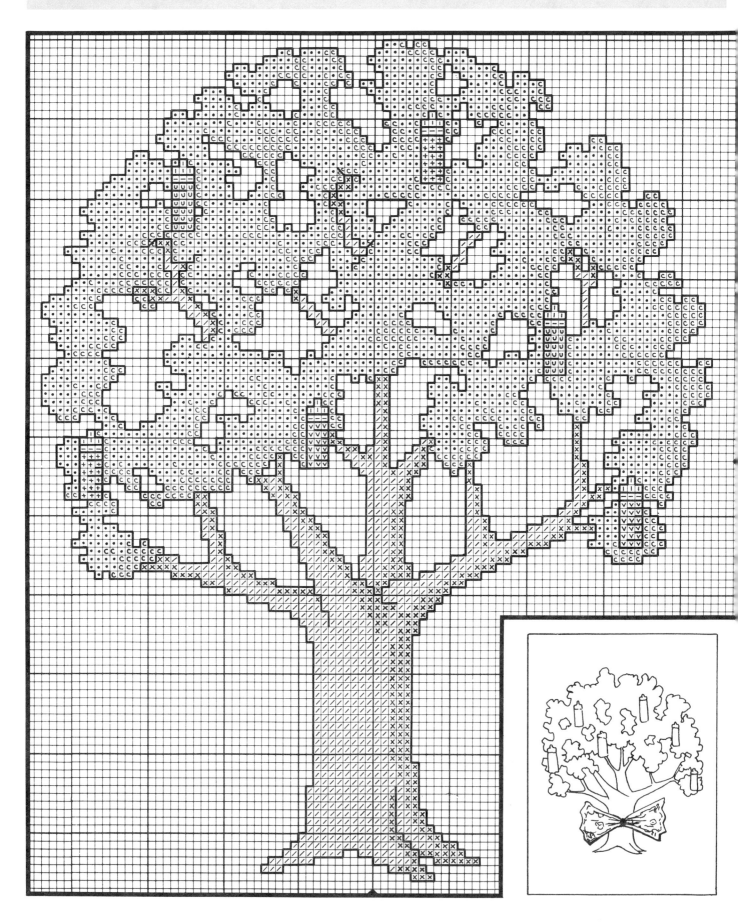

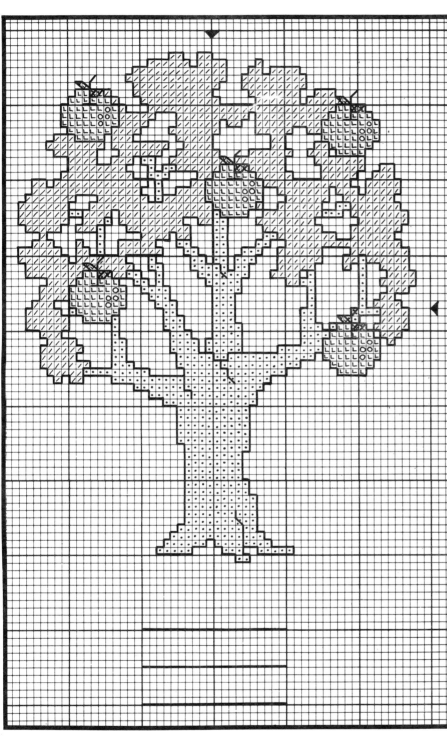

Teacher Tree

	DMC	ANCHOR	COLOR
o	White	2	White
╱	563	208	Jade Green
·	437	362	Tan
L	349	13	Dark Coral Red
v	907	255	Light Bright Green
	535	401	Very Dark Pewter Grey
	561	212	Very Dark Jade Green

Letters and numbers have been provided for personalization.
Use guidelines below tree to center letters and numbers.
Backstitch lettering in Very Dark Jade Green (2 strands).
All other backstitching is in Very Dark Pewter Grey.

New Arrival

	DMC	ANCHOR	COLOR
·	964	185	Light Seagreen
C	958	187	Dark Seagreen
╱	950	4146	Fawn Brown
X	407	882	Dark Fawn Brown
I	613	956	Light Chestnut Brown
−	White	2	White
v	745	300	Light Yellow
+	776	24	Baby Pink
U	827	159	Light True Blue
	844	401	Very Dark Grey

All backstitching is in Very Dark Grey.

See pages 52 and 53 for Alphabet.

Teacher Tree

Zweigart® Aida 14 Ct. Straw Gold
Floss Skeins
24 Tapestry Needle
Embroidery Hoop (optional)

Use 2 strands for cross stitching
Use 1 strand for backstitching
(unless otherwise indicated)
Stitch Count: 55w x 88h
Design Area Size: 3⅞" (9.8 cm) x 6¼" (15.9 cm)
Cut Fabric Size: 11⅞" (30.2 cm) x 14¼" (36.2 cm)
(allows 4" (10 cm) on all sides)

New Arrival

Zweigart® Jubliee 28 Ct. Carnation Pink
Floss Skeins
26 Tapestry Needles
Embroidery Hoop (optional)

Use 2 strands for cross stitching
Use 1 strand for backstitching
(unless otherwise indicated)
Stitch Over Two (to make 14 Ct.)
Stitch Count: 88w x 106h
Design Area Size: 6¼" (15.9 cm) x 7½" (19 cm)
Cut Fabric Size: 14¼" (36.2 cm) x 15½" (39.4 cm)
(allows 4" (10 cm) on all sides)

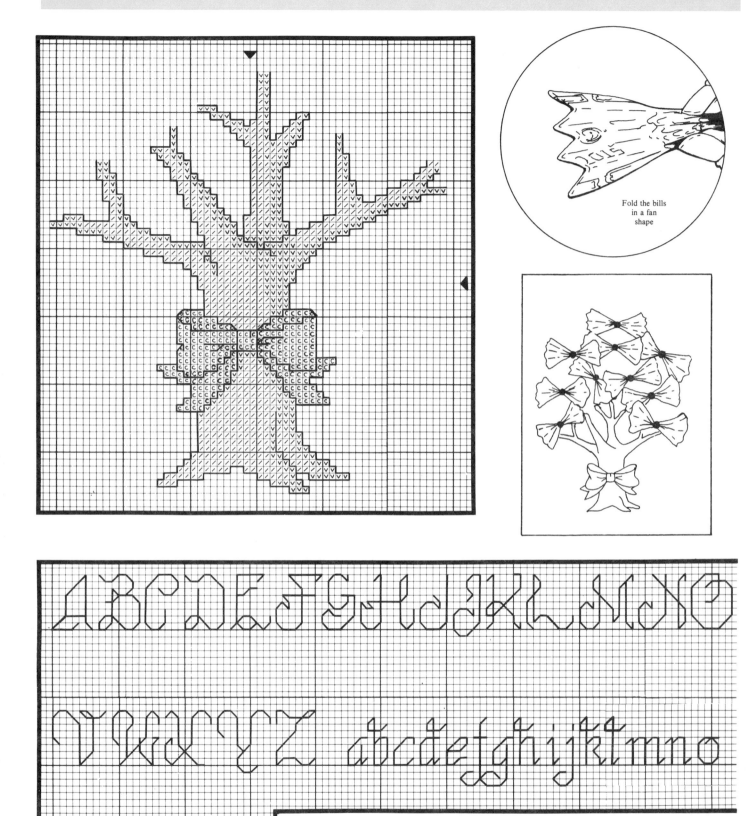

Fold the bills
in a fan
shape

Note:

On all money trees, the currency may be in any combination of bills depending upon how you want the total value of the gift to be (i.e. on the anniversary tree you have 12 spots, if you want the total value to be $100.00 USD, you could use 10 $5.00 bills and 5 $10.00 bills). The currency may be folded in a fan shape or rolled and tied with a ribbon. You may be as creative as you wish to be.

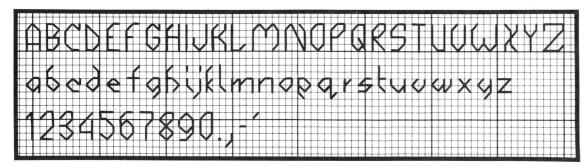

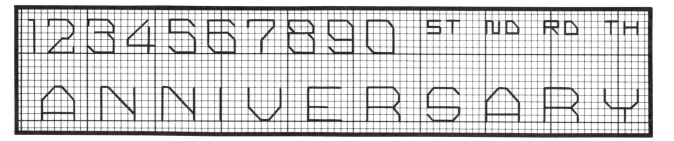

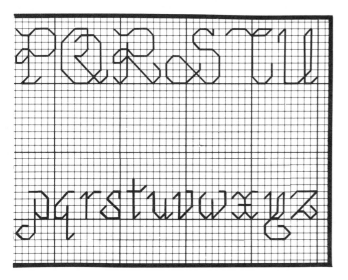

Materials

Zweigart® Annabelle 28 Ct. Dawn Grey
Floss Skeins, Blending filament
26 Tapestry Needle
Embroidery Hoop (optional)

Specifications

Use 2 strands for cross stitching
Use 1 strand for backstitching
(unless otherwise indicated)
Stitch Over Two (to make 14 Ct.)
Stitch Count: 60w x 62h
Design Area Size: 4¼" (10.8 cm) x 4½" (11.4 cm)
Cut Fabric Size: 12¼" (31.1 cm) x 12½" (31.7 cm)
(allows 4" (10 cm) on all sides)

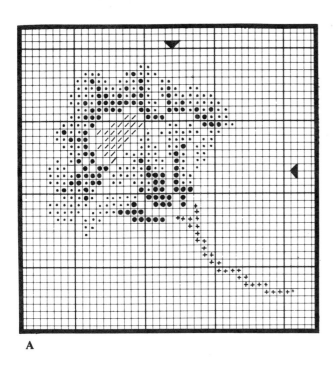

A

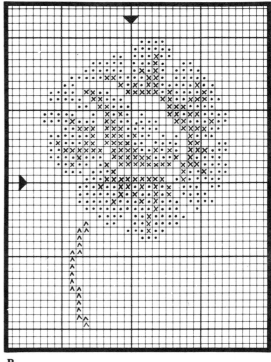

B

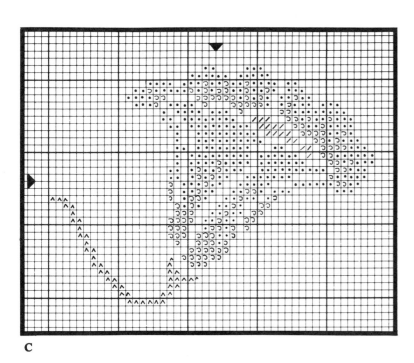

C

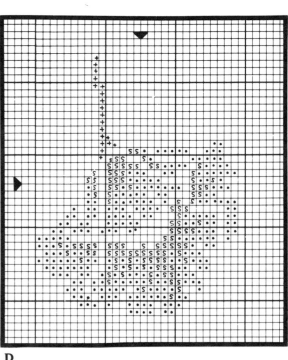

D

Stitch flowers on fabric as is
indicated in illustration below.

B	C	D	A	B	C	
D	A	B	C	D	A	
B	C	D	A	B	C	
D	A	B	C	D	A	
B	C	D	A	B	C	
D	A	B	C	D	A	
B	C	D	A	B	C	

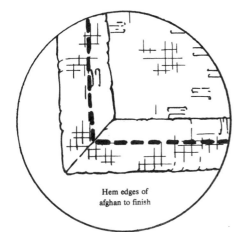

Hem edges of
afghan to finish

Legend

A

DMC	ANCHOR	COLOR
╱ 727	293	Light Topaz Yellow
• 754	778	Light Peach
● 758	868	Light Brick Red
+ 3363	861	Pine Green

B

DMC	ANCHOR	COLOR
• 3042	869	Light Antique Violet
✗ 3041	871	Antique Violet
ʌ 320	216	Light Soft Green

C

DMC	ANCHOR	COLOR
ɔ 402	347	Very Light Rust Brown
╱ 727	293	Light Topaz Yellow
• 945	347	Flesh Pink
ʌ 320	216	Light Soft Green

D

DMC	ANCHOR	COLOR
• 775	128	Very Light Baby Blue
S 932	920	Light Antique Blue
+ 3363	861	Pine Green

Stitch over two threads using 3 strands of floss.

Stitch flowers on fabric as is indicated in
illustration. Edges of fabric have been
hemmed to use as an afghan (lap blanket).

Materials

Zweigart® Honeycomb 18 Ct. White
Floss Skeins
24 Tapestry Needle
Embroidery Hoop (optional)

Specifications

Use 2 strands for cross stitching
Use 1 strand for backstitching
(unless otherwise indicated)
Stitch Over Two (to make 9 Ct.)
Finished Size: 42¾" (108.6 cm) x 52½" (1333.4 cm)

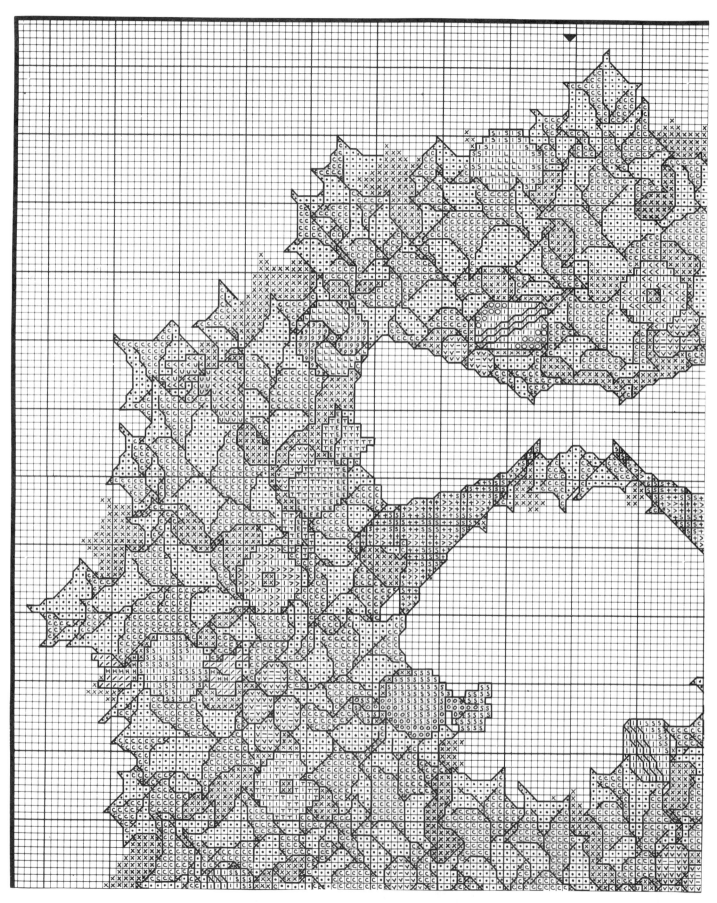

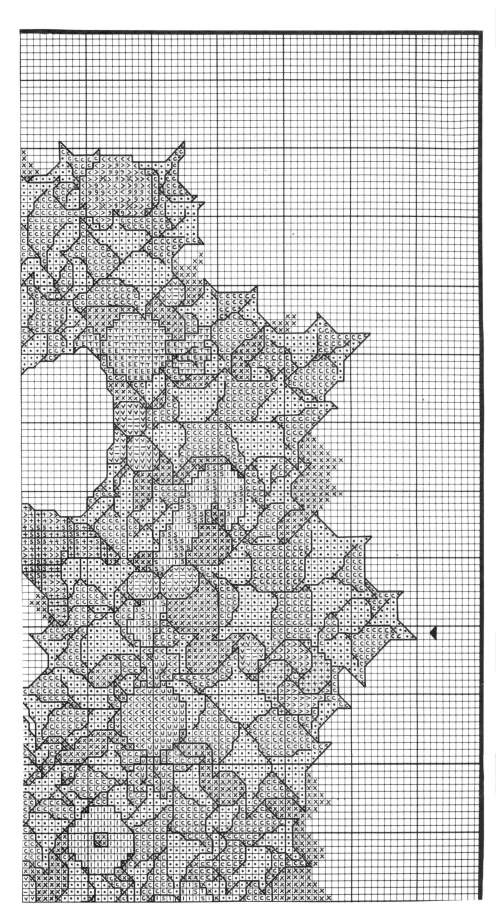

Legend

DMC	ANCHOR	COLOR
• 471	266	Light Avocado Green
c 470	267	Avocado Green
x 937	268	Very Dark Avocado Green
— 353	8	Peach
v 352	10	Dark Peach
I white	2	White
S 963	49	Light Dusty Pink
o 962	76	Dusty Pink
● 3064	914	Fawn Brown
T 3341	328	Light Apricot
E 3340	329	Apricot
+ 746	386	Soft White
> 3078	292	Baby Yellow
/ 3072	397	Light Pearl Grey
H 762	398	Very Light Steel Grey
L 964	185	Light Seagreen
9 959	186	Seagreen
< 3609	85	Light Plum Pink
U 3608	86	Plum Pink
801	357	Dark Brown

Balger® Pearl Blending filament is used throughout design to give a frosted look. Use 1 strand of Balger® with 2 strands of floss. Backstitch leaf veins in Very Dark Avocado Green.
Backstitch round candy spirals with the color used in the center. (2 strands)
Backstitch accent lines on peppermint patties in Light Dusty Pink.
Backstitch outside edges of leaves in Dark Brown.
Top portion of bow is stitched separately from design and is stitched on the bias. The backstitch accent lines are done in random order using Fawn Brown, Light Dusty Pink, Light Plum Pink. (2 strands)
The bow is then stiffened with sugar water or with a commercial fabric stiffener made for needlework. The bow is then cut out and glued in place.
An alphabet has been provided for use in personalizing your wreath sampler. Use 2 strands of Avocado Green for backstitch lettering.

Materials

Zweigart® Belfast 32 Ct. White
Floss Skeins/Blending filament
26 Tapestry Needle
Embroidery Hoop (optional)

Specifications

Use 2 strands for cross stitching
Use 1 strand for backstitching
(unless otherwise indicated)
Stitch Over Two (to make 16 Ct.)
Stitch Count: 163w x 169h
Design Area Size: 10⅛'' x (25.7 cm) x 10½'' (26.7 cm)
Cut Fabric Size: 18⅛'' (46 cm) x 18½'' (47 cm)
(allows 4'' (10 cm) on all sides)
You will need an 8'' (20.3 cm) square piece of fabric to stitch bow

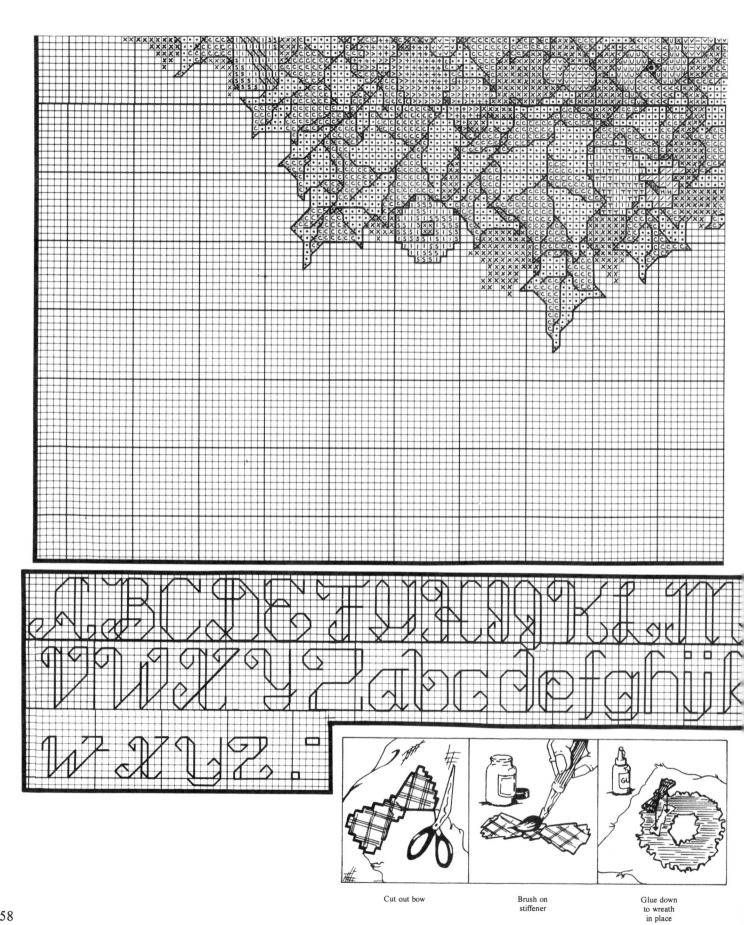

Cut out bow

Brush on
stiffener

Glue down
to wreath
in place

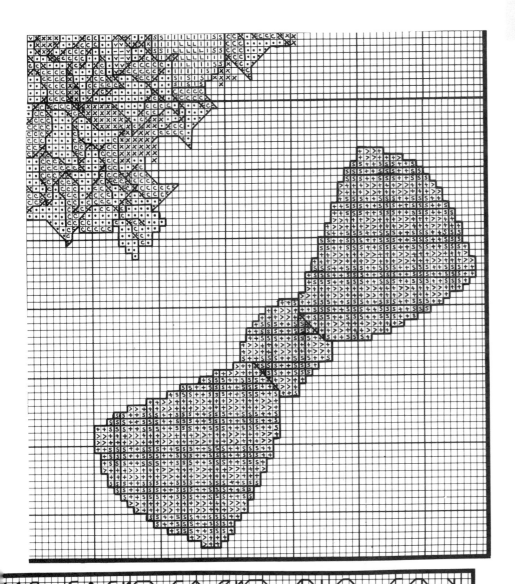

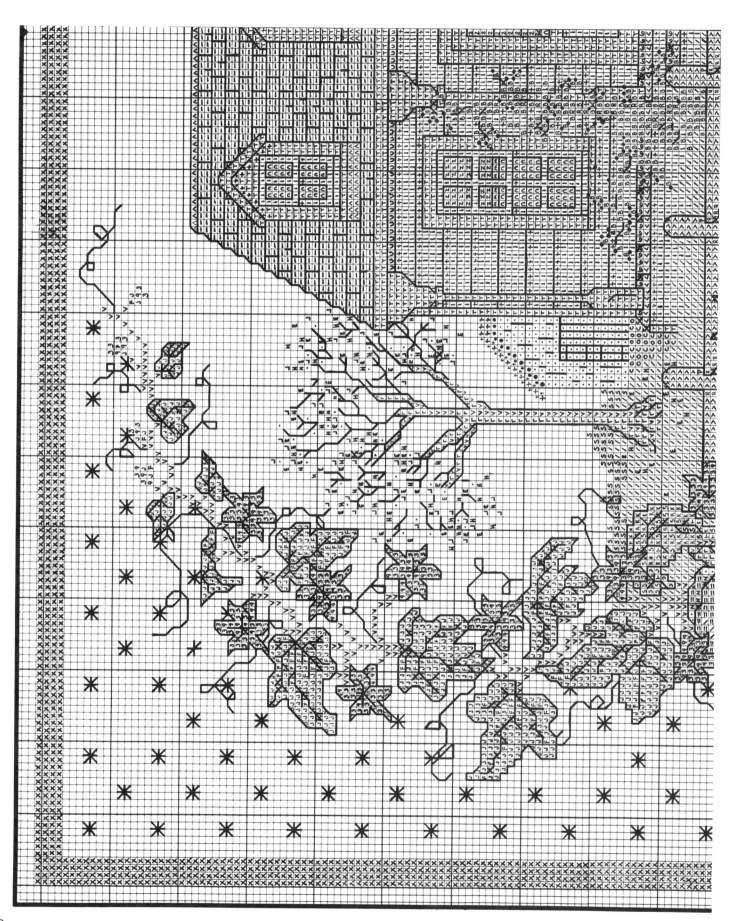

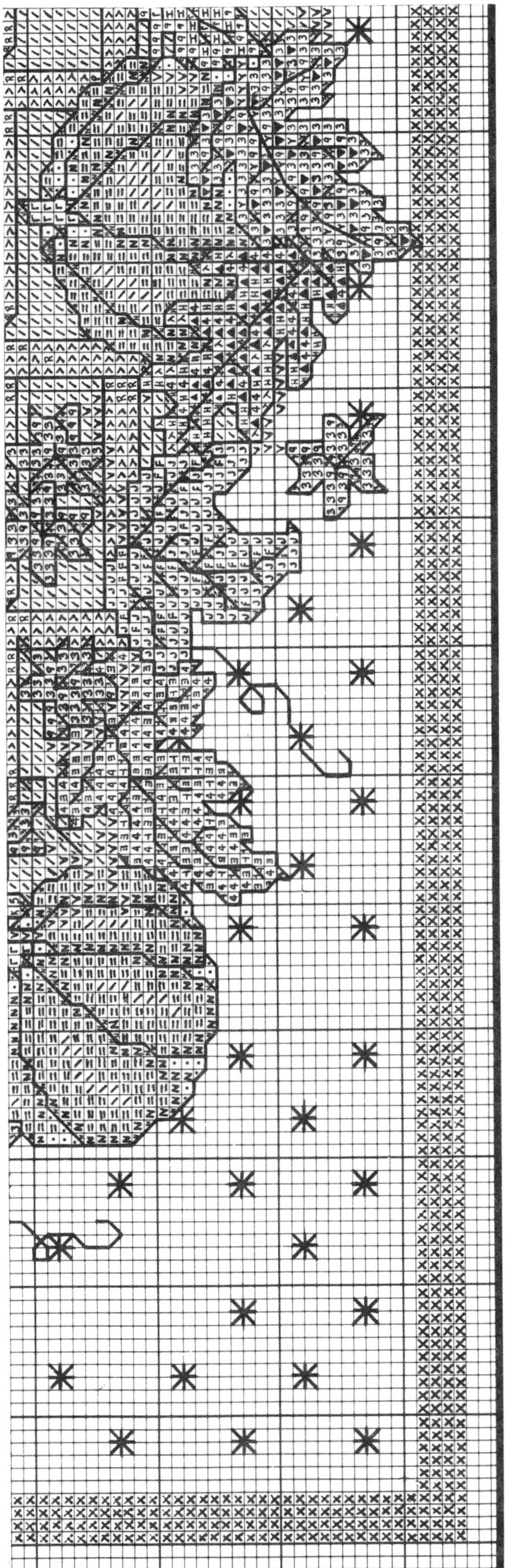

Legend

	DMC	ANCHOR	COLOR
+	745	300	Light Yellow
3	744	301	Yellow
▼	743	297	Dark Yellow
9	742	303	Light Tangerine
I	741	304	Tangerine
r	740	316	Dark Tangerine
6	3023	8581	Grey Brown
<	3022	830	Dark Grey Brown
\	722	323	Light Pumpkin
=	721	324	Pumpkin
/	524	858	Very Light Fern Green
L	523	859	Light Fern Green
S	522	862	Fern Green
N	921	349	Light Rust Red
•	919	341	Dark Rust Red
4	920	339	Rust Red
H	918	5968	Very Dark Rust Red
Z	739	885	Very Light Tan
M	738	942	Light Tan
⊣	946	332	Burnt Orange
∃	900	333	Dark Burnt Orange
C	372	887	Light Mustard Brown
O	371	888	Mustard Brown
Γ	420	375	Light Cinnamon
V	869	944	Cinnamon
J	989	242	Light Forest Green
F	987	244	Dark Forest Green
X	931	921	Antique Blue
>	612	832	Light Bark Brown
R	611	898	Bark Brown
P	610	889	Dark Bark Brown
K	3047	886	Light Straw Gold
5	3046	887	Straw Gold
ↄ	3045	373	Dark Straw Gold
┘	726	295	Topaz Yellow
T	White	2	White
⊢	733	280	Earth Green
I	762/W	397/2	Very Light Steel Grey/White

(continued on next page)

Materials

Zweigart® Lugana 25 Ct. Cream
Floss Skeins, Marlitt, Metallics, Blending filaments
26 Tapestry Needle
Embroidery Hoop (optional)

Specifications

Use 2 strands for cross stitching
Use 1 strand for backstitching
(unless otherwise indicated)
Stitch Over Two (to make 12½ Ct.)
Stitch Count: 236w x 136h
Design Area Size: 18⅞" (47.9 cm) x 10⅞" (27.6 cm)
Cut Fabric Size: 26⅞" (68.3 cm) x 18⅞" (47.9 cm)
(allows 4" (10 cm) on all sides)

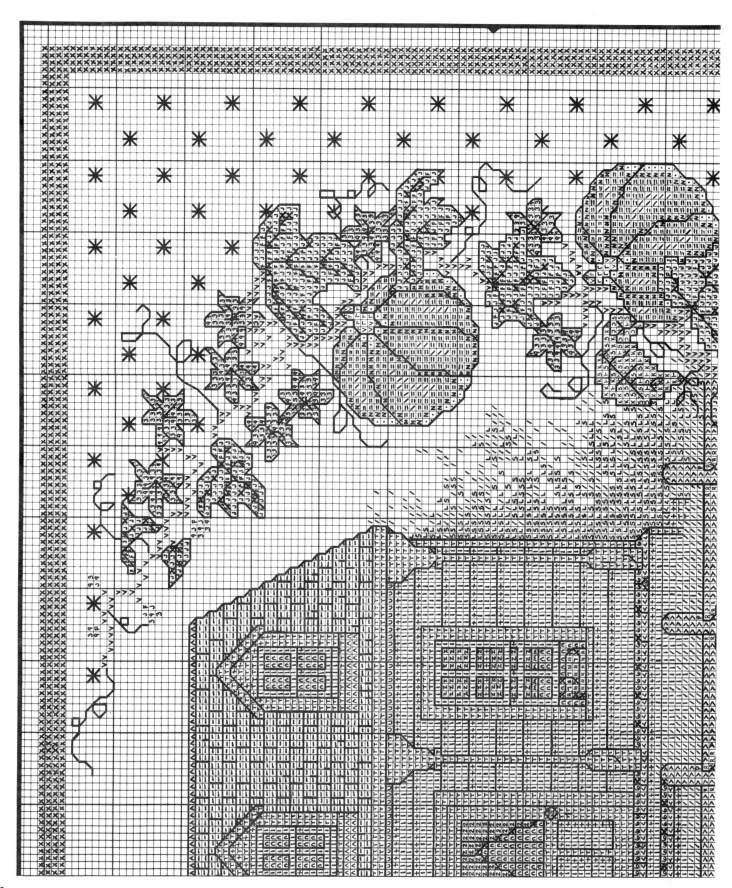

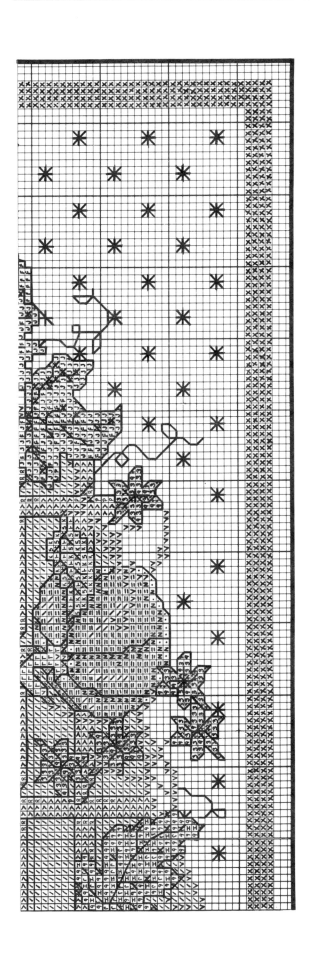

(continued)

	DMC	ANCHOR	COLOR
U	415	398	Light Steel Grey
Y	470	267	Avocado Green
B	937	268	Very Dark Avocado Green
∩	3325	159	Light Baby Blue
●	355	5968	Dark Brick Red
E	783	307	Light Topaz Gold
∧	839	380	Dark Beige Brown
−	840	379	Beige Brown
▲	817	19	Very Dark Coral Red
λ	300	352	Dark Rust Brown
2	3078	292	Baby Yellow
⊥	3031	905	Dark Mocha Brown
‖	648	900	Light Beaver Grey
⌐	647	8581	Beaver Grey
	970	316	Orange
	844	401	Very Dark Grey

French Knots for center of pumpkin flowers are in Pumpkin. (1 strand)
French Knots for berries on bush in front of house are in Orange. (1 strand)
Backstitch vine feelers in Cinnamon.
All other backstitching is in Very Dark Grey.
The large symbol (✳) on graph in Light Baby Blue is an Algerian Eye Stitch stitched over two threads.

See Page 67 for Algerian Eye Stitch instructions.

Materials

See Page 61

Specifications

See Page 61

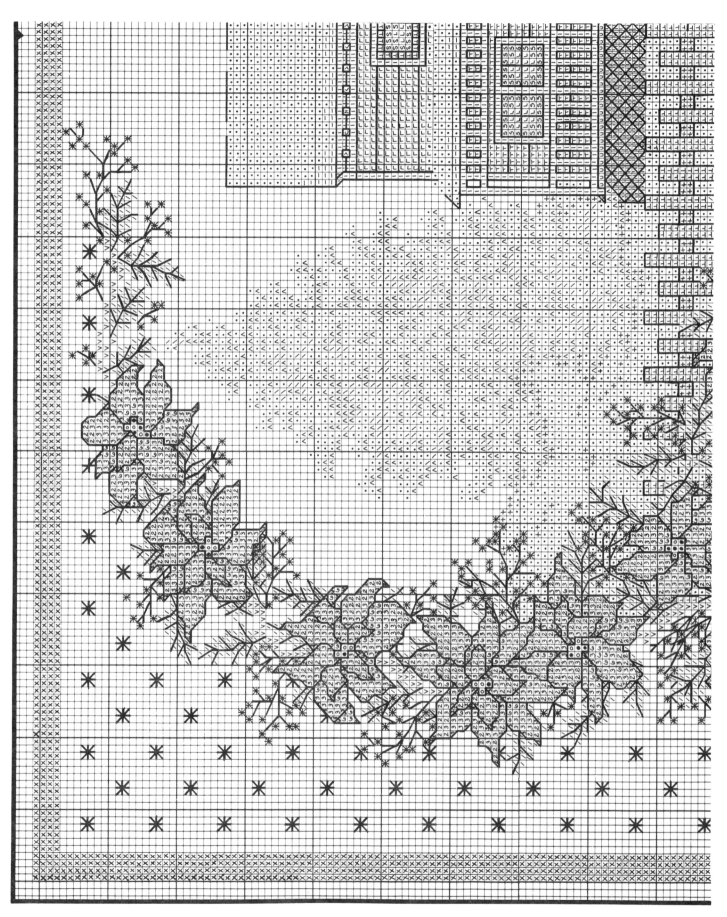

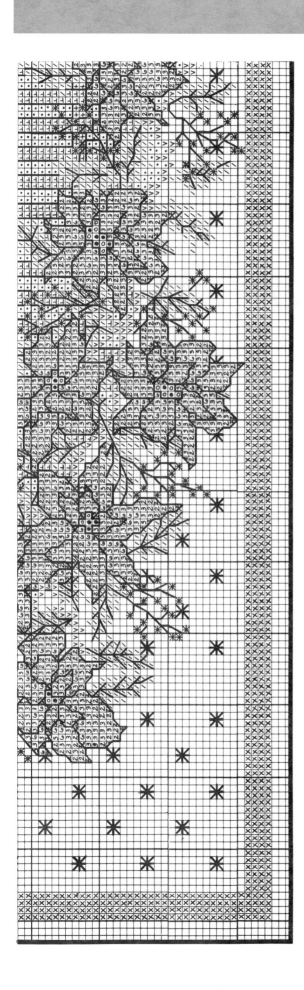

Legend

DMC ANCHOR COLOR

	DMC	ANCHOR	COLOR
•	WM	2	White/WM
I	White	2	White
>	666	46	Christmas Red
c	700	229	Christmas Green
N	444	291	Lemon Yellow
⌐	775	128	Very Light Baby Blue
<	334	145	Baby Blue
V	435	369	Very Light Brown
X	931	921	Antique Blue
S	745	300	Light Yellow
L	746	386	Soft White
T	822	387	Light Grey Beige
II	842	376	Very Light Beige Brown
U	644	830	Beige Brown
●	3348	265	Very Light Hunter Green
\	3347	266	Light Hunter Green
^	3346	257	Hunter Green
−	747	158	Light Sky Blue
+	3072	397	Light Pearl Grey
/	988	243	Forest Green
o	727	293	Light Topaz Yellow
2	352	10	Dark Peach
3	350	11	Coral Red
6	817	19	Very Dark Coral Red
⊥	648	900	Beaver Grey
	GM		Gold Metallic
	986	246	Very Dark Forest Green
	3031	905	Dark Mocha Brown
	3325	159	Light Baby Blue
	304	47	Red

WM indicated the use of White Marlitt.
GM indicates the use of Balger® Gold Metallic.
French Knots on Christmas tree are in Gold
Metallic. (1 strand)
Backstitch veins in holly leaves in Very Dark
Forest Green.
Backstitch bow on door in Christmas Red.
(2 strands)
Backstitch branches (of Red Algerian Eye Stitch
flowers) in Very Light Brown.

(continued on next page)

Materials

See Page 61

Specifications

See Page 61

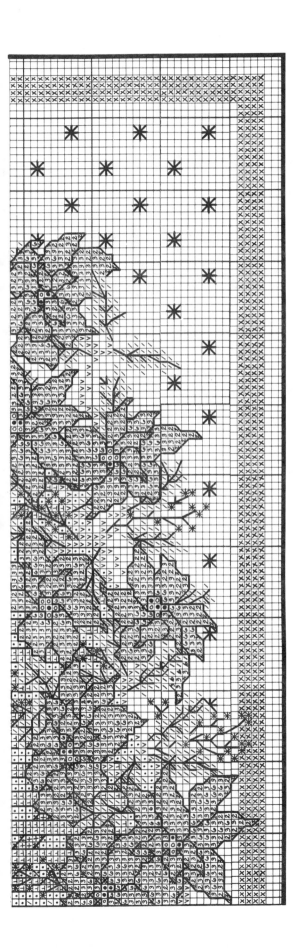

Legend

(continued)

All other backstitching is in Dark Mocha Brown.
The small symbol (✳) on graph in Red are small
Algerian Eye Stitches. Use 1 strand.
The large symbol (✵) on graph in Light Baby
Blue is an Algerian Eye Stitch, stitched over
two threads. Please see illustrations on this page.

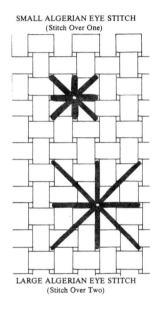

SMALL ALGERIAN EYE STITCH
(Stitch Over One)

LARGE ALGERIAN EYE STITCH
(Stitch Over Two)

Materials

See Page 61

Specifications

See Page 61

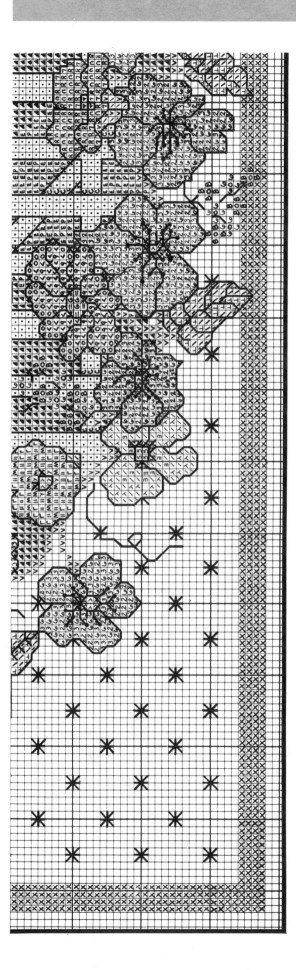

Legend

	DMC	ANCHOR	COLOR
X	931	921	Antique Blue
•	White	2	White
+	746	386	Soft White
I	356	5975	Brick Red
L	3033	388	Light Mocha Brown
S	3032	903	Mocha Brown
J	407	882	Fawn Brown
∧	632	936	Dark Fawn Brown
U	3024	900	Light Grey Brown
■	3023	8581	Grey Brown
C	762	397	Very Light Grey
N	3364	843	Light Pine Green
H	3363	861	Pine Green
∩	353	8	Peach
R	352	10	Dark Peach
◢	471	266	Light Avocado Green
Z	469	267	Dark Avocado Green
E	613	956	Very Light Bark Brown
P	612	832	Light Bark Brown
T	3325	159	Light Baby Blue
B	334	145	Baby Blue
****	3347	266	Light Hunter Green
5	745	300	Light Yellow
o	744	301	Yellow
<	743	297	Dark Yellow
G	437	362	Tan
=	435	369	Very Light Brown
⊥	3346	257	Hunter Green
V	3345	268	Dark Hunter Green
2	818	48	Light Baby Pink
6	776	24	Baby Pink
3	899	27	Dark Baby Pink
Y	445	288	Light Lemon Yellow
>	444	291	Lemon Yellow
M	333	119	Blue Violet
Γ	794	120	Light Cornflower Blue
II	793	121	Cornflower Blue
−	746/W	386/2	Soft White/White
q	742	303	Light Tangerine
/	211	108	Very Light Lavender
λ	210	104	Light Lavender
Ǝ	209	105	Lavender
▼	3371	382	Black Brown

(continued on next page)

Materials

See Page 61

Specifications

See Page 61

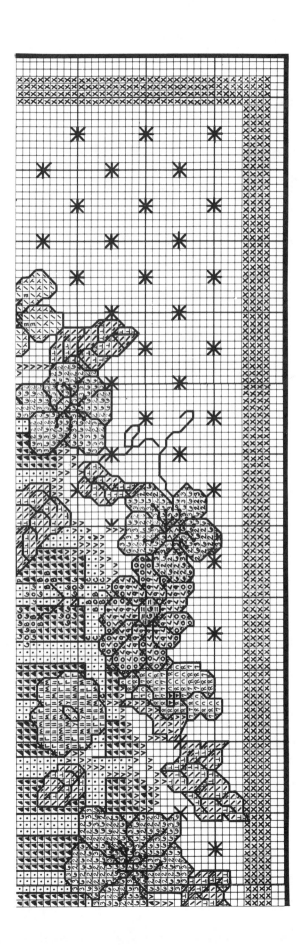

(continued)

DMC ANCHOR COLOR

7 350 11 Coral Red
309 42 Carnation Red
3031 905 Dark Mocha Brown

The symbol (—) uses 1 strand of Soft White and 1 strand of White.
French Knots for Pink Wild Roses are in Carnation Red. (2 strands)
Backstitch gate latch handle in Black Brown.
Backstitch vine and leaf in Dark Hunter Green. (2 strands)
Backstitch center of Pink Wild Roses in Lemon Yellow. (2 strands)
Backstitch center of Violets in Blue Violet. (2 strands)
All flower edges are backstitched in Very Dark Grey.
All other backstitching is in Dark Mocha Brown.
The large symbol (✳) on graph in Light Baby Blue is an Algerian Eye Stitch, stitched over two threads.
See Page 67 for Algerian Eye Stitch instructions.

Materials

See Page 61

Specification

See Page 61

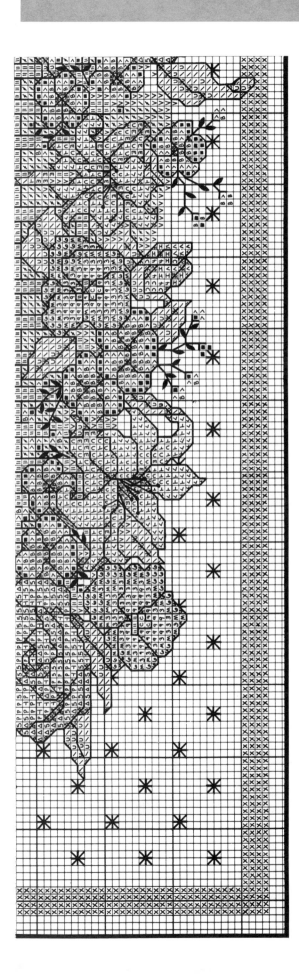

Legend

	DMC	ANCHOR	COLOR
X	931	921	Antique Blue
B	775	128	Very Light Baby Blue
>	3325	159	Light Baby Blue
■	334	145	Baby Blue
\	470	267	Avocado Green
U	469	268	Dark Avocado Green
6	210	104	Light Lavender
3	209	105	Lavender
M	208	110	Dark Lavender
II	White	2	White
C	307	289	Lemon Yellow
<	743	297	Dark Yellow
⊢	742	303	Light Tangerine
∩	741	304	Tangerine
∃	740	316	Dark Tangerine
△	819	892	Ultra Light Baby Pink
5	818	48	Very Light Baby Pink
P	776	24	Light Baby Pink
⊣	3326	25	Baby Pink
∧	899	27	Dark Baby Pink
T	746	386	Soft White
−	747	158	Light Sky Blue
L	739	885	Very Light Tan
Z	738	942	Light Tan
⊥	437	362	Tan
S	436	363	Dark Tan
⌐	948	778	Very Light Peach
+	3072	397	Light Pearl Grey
G	3047	886	Light Straw Gold
N	3046	887	Straw Gold
⁄	3348	265	Light Hunter Green
R	3345	268	Dark Hunter Green
V	895	246	Very Dark Hunter Green
2	435	369	Very Light Brown
=	434	309	Light Brown
⌐	907	255	Light Bright Green
H	906	256	Bright Green
E	905	258	Dark Bright Green

(continued on next page)

Materials

See Page 61

Specifications

See Page 61

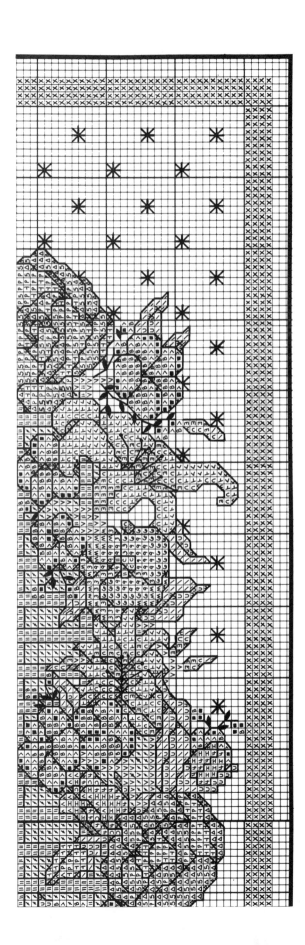

Legend

(continued)

	DMC	ANCHOR	COLOR
Ⲓ	335	41	Light Carnation Red
4	309	42	Carnation Red
Ⴖ	326	59	Dark Carnation Red
o	554	96	Light Violet
▲	553	98	Violet
▼	552	101	Dark Violet
٩	550	112	Very Dark Violet
•	3024	900	Light Grey Brown
κ	3023	8581	Grey Brown
●	3022	382	Dark Grey Brown
	3031	905	Dark Mocha Brown
	801	357	Dark Brown
	3325	159	Light Baby Blue

French Knots for Day Lilies are in Dark Mocha Brown. (1 strand)
Backstitch leaf veins and flower bud stems in Dark Hunter Green.
Backstitch birds in Dark Brown. (2 strands)
🖉 indicates the use of Lazy Daisy Stitch using Very Dark Hunter Green. See illustration on this page.
The large symbol (✳) on graph in Light Baby Blue is an Algerian Eye Stitch, stitched over two threads. Please see illustration on Page 61.
The symbol (/) in windows indicate the use of a half cross stitch for all windows in Light Pearl Grey.
See Page 67 for Algerian Eye Stitch instructions.

LAZY DAISY (also known as Detached Chain)
Can cover any number of squares; shown here covering 16. Made up of 4-6 pairs of stitches. Bring needle up at the center of the daisy ''1''. Re-insert needle into ''1'', immediately slipping needle through ''2'', careful to keep thread under needle's point. Complete with a tiny stitch, radiating outward, according to the chart.

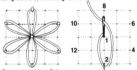

One completed Lazy Daisy

Materials

See Page 61

Specifications

See Page 61

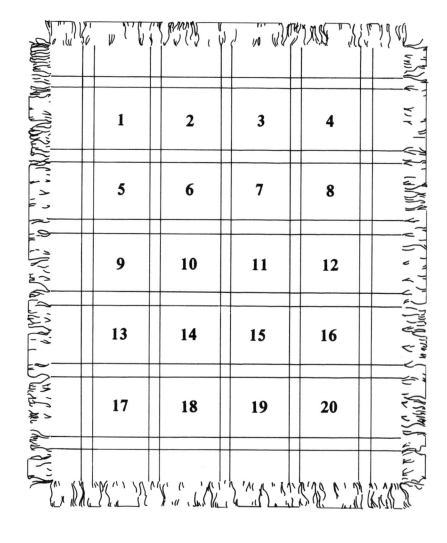

1	2	3	4
5	6	7	8
9	10	11	12
13	14	15	16
17	18	19	20

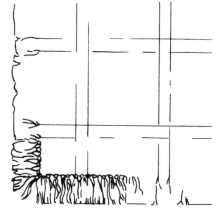

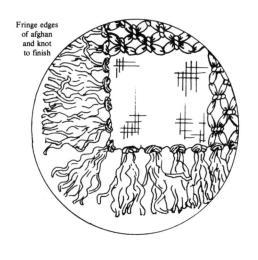

Fringe edges
of afghan
and knot
to finish

Zweigart® Novara 14 Ct. Beige or
Zweigart® Hearthside 14 Ct. Blue
Floss Skeins
24 Tapestry Needle
Embroidery Hoop (optional)

Use 2 strands for cross stitching
Use 1 strand for backstitching
(unless otherwise indicated)
Stitch Count: 95w x 95h each square
Cut Fabric Size: 1⅓ yards (1.2 m)

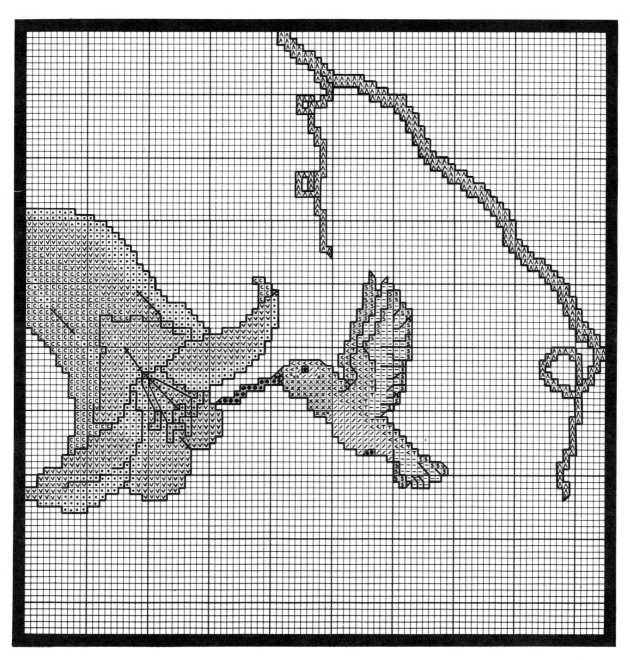

1. Hummingbird

	DMC	ANCHOR	COLOR
+	676	891	Old Gold
c	742	303	Light Tangerine
v	741	304	Tangerine
•	740	316	Dark Tangerine
/	White	2	White
T	471	266	Light Avocado Green
<	472	264	Avocado Green
X	606	335	Bright Orange
—	3024	900	Light Grey Brown
S	3022	8581	Grey Brown
●	844	401	Very Dark Grey
Λ	732	281	Green

Use long stitch for pistils in the flower using Very Dark Grey.
All backstitching is in Very Dark Grey.

2. Common Flicker

	DMC	ANCHOR	COLOR
–	White	2	White
>	415	398	Light Steel Grey
o	414	400	Steel Grey
I	413	401	Dark Steel Grey
/	436	363	Brown
+	402	347	Light Rust Brown
Z	606	335	Bright Orange
C	647	8581	Beaver Grey
U	725	306	Topaz Yellow
X	844	401	Very Dark Grey
T	840	379	Beige Brown
S	368	240	Light Soft Green
V	320	216	Soft Green
Λ	732	281	Earth Green
●	225	892	Light Shell Pink
\	340	118	Blue Violet
L	211	108	Light Lavender

French Knot for eye is in Very Dark Grey.
All backstitching is in Very Dark Grey.

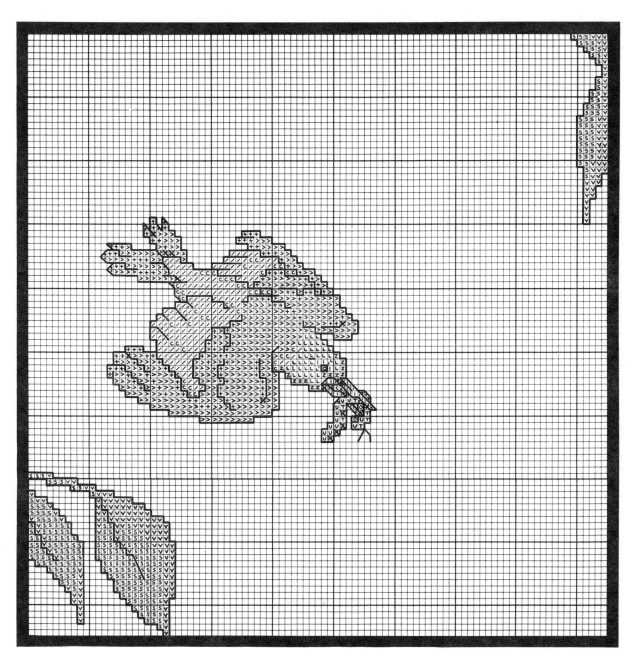

3. Red-headed Woodpecker

	DMC	ANCHOR	COLOR
S	368	240	Light Soft Green
V	320	216	Soft Green
O	435	369	Brown
/	White	2	White
C	822	387	Light Grey Beige
>	844	401	Very Dark Grey
+	648	900	Light Beaver Grey
L	350	11	Coral Red
Z	817	19	Dark Coral Red
I	318	399	Steel Grey
<	414	400	Dark Steel Grey
U	733	280	Earth Green
T	732	281	Dark Earth Green

French Knot for eye is in Very Dark Grey.
All other backstitching is in Very Dark Grey.

4. Fork-tailed Flycatcher

	DMC	ANCHOR	COLOR
•	White	2	White
S	368	240	Light Soft Green
V	320	216	Soft Green
/	312	147	Navy Blue
+	648	900	Light Beaver Grey
I	743	297	Dark Yellow
X	844	401	Very Dark Grey
>	924	851	Dark Blue Grey
Z	839	380	Dark Beige Brown

All backstitching is in Very Dark Grey.

5. Scissor-tailed Flycatcher

	DMC	ANCHOR	COLOR
+	318	399	Steel Grey
·	413	401	Dark Steel Grey
●	301	349	Rust Brwon
I	801	357	Brown
L	White	2	White
o	352	10	Dark Peach
V	758	868	Light Brick Red
C	844	401	Very Dark Grey
S	746	386	Soft White
<	932	920	Light Antique Blue
T	931	921	Antique Blue
>	676	891	Old Gold
X	935	862	Dark Avocado Green
/	3363	861	Pine Green
−	3032	903	Mocha Brown
U	611	898	Bark Brown

All backstitching is in Very Dark Grey.

6. Blue Jay

	DMC	ANCHOR	COLOR
L	White	2	White
S	318	399	Steel Grey
•	413	401	Dark Steel Grey
⟩	813	160	True Blue
T	826	161	Dark True Blue
C	844	401	Very Dark Grey
—	3032	903	Mocha Brown
U	611	898	Bark Brown
X	935	862	Dark Avocado Green
⁄	3363	861	Pine Green

All backstitching is in Very Dark Grey.

7. Chestnut-backed Chickadee

DMC	ANCHOR	COLOR		DMC	ANCHOR	COLOR
• 931	921	Antique Blue		I 367	216	Soft Green
● 434	309	Brown		∩ 605	50	Cranberry Pink
V 976	308	Cinnamon		∧ 600	59	Cranberry Red
Z 975	355	Dark Cinnamon				
T 648	900	Light Beaver Grey				
+ 646	8581	Dark Beaver Grey		All backstitching is in Very Dark Grey.
o 676	891	Old Gold				
C 844	401	Very Dark Grey				
L White	2	White				
/ 3363	861	Pine Green				
X 935	862	Dark Avocado Green				
— 3032	903	Mocha Brown				
U 611	898	Bark Brown				
S 3021	382	Dark Grey Brown				
< 520	846	Dark Fern Green				

8. Barn Swallow

	DMC	ANCHOR	COLOR
U	611	898	Bark Brown
S	3021	382	Dark Grey Brown
L	932	920	Antique Blue
●	434	309	Brown
I	729	890	Old Gold
X	680	901	Dark Old Gold
+	White	2	White
/	921	349	Rust Red
C	919	341	Dark Rust Red
V	844	401	Very Dark Grey
O	745	300	Yellow
<	704	256	Light Christmas Green
\	520	846	Fern Green
∧	600	59	Cranberry Red
∩	605	50	Cranberry Pink
−	318	399	Steel Grey
•	414	400	Dark Steel Grey

All backstitching is in Very Dark Grey.

9. Red-breasted Nuthatch

	DMC	ANCHOR	COLOR
•	402	347	Light Rust Brown
o	726	295	Topaz Yellow
L	White	2	White
I	318	399	Steel Grey
−	807	168	Light Ocean Blue
●	806	169	Dark Ocean Blue
T	936	269	Dark Forest Green
V	3031	905	Dark Mocha Brown
+	746	386	Soft White
/	3363	861	Pine Green
z	976	308	Cinnamon
S	610	889	Bark Brown
<	844	401	Very Dark Grey
C	469	267	Avocado Green
X	935	862	Dark Avocado Green

All backstitching is in Very Dark Grey.

10. Robin

	DMC	ANCHOR	COLOR
—	722	324	Light Rust Red
o	921	349	Rust Red
●	400	351	Rust Brown
I	White	2	White
•	743	297	Dark Yellow
+	415	398	Light Steel Grey
U	648	900	Light Beaver Grey
Z	646	8581	Beaver Grey
<	844	401	Very Dark Grey
/	3363	861	Pine Green
T	936	269	Forest Green
S	610	889	Bark Brown
V	3031	905	Mocha Brown
C	469	267	Avocado Green
X	935	862	Dark Avocado Green
>	839	380	Dark Beige Brown

All backstitching is in Very Dark Grey.

11. Cardinal

	DMC	ANCHOR	COLOR
I	351	11	Light Coral Red
•	349	13	Dark Coral Red
V	3031	905	Mocha Brown
+	844	401	Very Dark Grey
●	304	47	Red
<	725	306	Dark Topaz Yellow
L	783	307	Light Topaz Gold
>	400	351	Rust Brown
C	469	267	Avocado Green
T	936	269	Forest Green
U	611	898	Bark Brown
S	610	889	Dark Bark Brown
—	3021	382	Dark Grey Brown
/	367	216	Soft Green
X	520	846	Dark Fern Green
∩	605	50	Cranberry Pink

	DMC	ANCHOR	COLOR
∧	600	59	Cranberry Red
o	White	2	White

All backstitching is in Very Dark Grey.

12. Townsend's Warbler

	DMC	ANCHOR	COLOR
•	519	167	Sky Blue
●	435	369	Brown
O	645	905	Dark Beaver Grey
+	415	398	Steel Grey
L	White	2	White
V	844	401	Very Dark Grey
<	831	889	Green Gold
—	726	295	Topaz Yellow
I	977	307	Cinnamon
X	520	846	Dark Fern Green
/	367	216	Soft Green
U	611	898	Bark Brown
S	3021	382	Dark Grey Brown
∩	605	50	Cranberry Pink
^	600	59	Cranberry Red

All backstitching is in Very Dark Grey.

13. Oriole

	DMC	ANCHOR	COLOR
•	931	921	Antique Blue
●	898	360	Dark Brown
−	726	295	Topaz Yellow
+	725	306	Dark Topaz Yellow
S	White	2	White
<	844	401	Very Dark Grey
X	936	269	Forest Green
C	469	267	Avocado Green
╱	610	889	Bark Brown
V	3031	905	Mocha Brown

All backstitching is in Very Dark Grey.

14. Cardinal

	DMC	ANCHOR	COLOR
+	676	891	Light Old Gold
o	729	890	Old Gold
c	726	295	Topaz Yellow
—	351	11	Light Coral Red
X	349	13	Dark Coral Red
I	742	303	Light Tangerine
<	740	316	Dark Tangerine
L	815	43	Dark Red
>	839	380	Beige Brown
T	469	267	Avocado Green
U	936	269	Forest Green
/	610	889	Bark Brown
V	3031	905	Mocha Brown

French knot for cherry is in Very Dark Grey.
All backstitching is in Very Dark Grey.

15. Blue-grey Gnatcatcher

	DMC	ANCHOR	COLOR
o	932	920	Light Antique Blue
●	844	401	Very Dark Grey
I	827	159	Light True Blue
S	826	161	True Blue
–	White	2	White
+	415	398	Steel Grey
c	349	13	Dark Coral Red
L	815	43	Dark Red
>	839	380	Dark Beige Brown
T	469	267	Avocado Green
U	936	269	Forest Green
/	610	889	Bark Brown
V	3031	905	Mocha Brown

French knot for cherry is in Very Dark Grey.
All backstitching is in Very Dark Grey.

16. Scarlet Tanager

	DMC	ANCHOR	COLOR
•	844	401	Very Dark Grey
−	726	295	Topaz Yellow
V	350	11	Coral Red
+	349	13	Dark Coral Red
T	469	267	Avocado Green
U	936	269	Forest Green
I	611	898	Bark Brown
S	3021	382	Dark Grey Brown
/	367	216	Soft Green
X	520	846	Dark Fern Green

All backstitching is in Very Dark Grey.

17. Red-winged Blackbird

	DMC	ANCHOR	COLOR
C	469	267	Avocado Green
X	936	269	Forest Green
I	White	2	White
O	318	399	Light Steel Grey
/	414	400	Steel Grey
•	413	401	Dark Steel Grey
Z	434	309	Brown
−	726	295	Topaz Yellow
+	844	401	Very Dark Grey
U	3072	397	Light Pearl Grey
V	350	11	Coral Red

All backstitching is in Very Dark Grey.

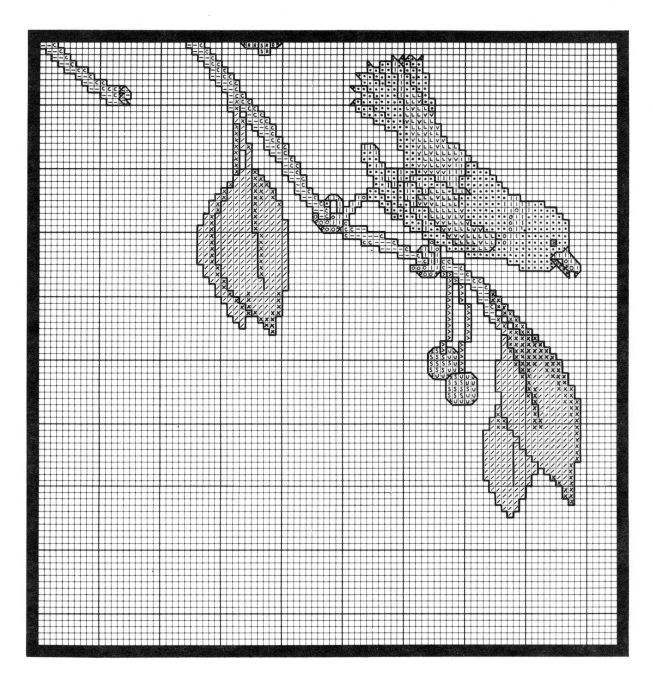

18. Bobolink

	DMC	ANCHOR	COLOR
R	351	11	Light Coral Red
S	349	13	Dark Coral Red
U	815	43	Dark Red
o	436	363	Light Brown
Z	434	309	Brown
•	844	401	Very Dark Grey
I	676	891	Old Gold
>	839	380	Beige Brown
V	644	830	Grey Beige
L	White	2	White
/	469	267	Avocado Green
X	936	269	Forest Green
—	610	889	Bark Brown
C	3031	905	Mocha Brown

All backstitching is in Very Dark Grey.

19. Yellow-throated Vireo

	DMC	ANCHOR	COLOR
L	472	264	Light Avocado Green
X	470	267	Avocado Green
>	453	397	Light Pearl Grey
+	451	399	Dark Pearl Grey
V	844	401	Very Dark Grey
C	White	2	White
I	318	399	Steel Grey
S	647	8581	Beaver Grey
/	744	301	Yellow
T	833	874	Green Gold
—	945	347	Flesh Pink
O	433	371	Brown
•	801	357	Dark Brown

All backstitching is in Very Dark Grey.

20. Bluebird

	DMC	ANCHOR	COLOR
L	472	264	Light Avocado Green
X	470	267	Avocado Green
/	367	216	Soft Green
Z	520	846	Dark Fern Green
o	White	2	White
U	415	398	Light Steel Grey
I	414	400	Steel Grey
R	312	147	Light Navy Blue
V	334	145	Baby Blue
S	350	11	Coral Red
H	353	8	Peach
−	775	128	Light Baby Blue
E	815	43	Dark Red
T	434	309	Brown
●	844	401	Very Dark Grey
·	611	898	Bark Brown
>	610	889	Dark Bark Brown

	DMC	ANCHOR	COLOR
+	3033	388	Light Mocha Brown
<	946	332	Bright Orange
C	522	859	Fern Green

All backstitching is in Very Dark Grey.